MW00876223

Praise for *The Progenitors*

To say Andrew Antijo has a powerful imagination is too meek. His is working on some sort of high octane fuel for sure. From international venues and intrigue to the lowly docks of Cleveland, Ohio, from the Baltic Sea to Lake Erie, while bringing to life '...the prodigies in the dog world,' these stories are a fun and ruckus 'tour de force' of dog prowess and adventure. The author weaves many good stories. Ann! Get me a Bud! gets the creativity award from me. In short, I was quite impressed and amused.
Tom

A note to the author: All of our dog loving friends in Bay Village have read and enjoyed your excellent stories about Deuce's ancestors. Sorry to have kept your new book so long, but more and more folks wanted to read it!
Jerry and Susie

I'm loving this book! Thanks for sharing.
Ann

AMERICAN KENNEL CLUB · FOUNDED 1884

Certified Pedigree

THE PROGENITORS OF
DEUCE CLARENCE JONES

DEUCE CLARENCE JONES
SR51552609
LABRADOR RETRIEVER MALE CHLT
Date Whelped: 03/10/2008

Sire SKAGGS' WESTWOOD GUS
SN79902703 (12-06) CHLT

TENDERCARE BUBBLING BUCKEYE
SN45717701 t(10-00) OFA38G OFEL71 CHLT
AKC DNA #V253027

BUBBLING BEDOUINE
SN43476201 (08-97) CHLT (FIN)

TENDERCARE MUSKELUNGE DEBBIE
SN12144001 (01-97) OFA25G BLK

ABBEYGAYLE MAD RIVER SWIMMER
SN46773706 (03-01) CHLT

CLIFTON HILL DUCKBOAT GUNNER
SN11278507 (10-95) OFA30F CHLT AKC DNA
#V200610

CONSTANCE OF VALENTINE
SN31130102 (10-97) CHLT

Dam CHOCOLATE MOLLY II
SN93194702 (05-04) CHLT

MURRAY'S MOCHA MACK
SN79976003 (01-03) CHLT

DOUBLE D REESES PIECES
SN85983803 (03-01) OFA46G CHLT AKC DNA
#V471596

DOUBLE D MOCHA DELIGHT
SN61368803 (03-01) CHLT

ANN HEUSER
SN66455803 (03-01) OFA25G CHLT

COCO RODERECUS REID
SN30702110 (06-98) CHLT

HOLLY BERRY OLIVEIRA
SN22299501 (06-98) CHLT

Executive Secretary

The Seal of The American Kennel Club affixed hereto certifies that this pedigree was compiled from official Stud Book records on April 13, 2009.

AMERICAN KENNEL CLUB®

ADVENTURES OF DEUCE CLARENCE JONES

BOOK I—THE PROGENITORS

by Andrew Antijo

ISBN: 978-1-4834-5171-8 (sc)
ISBN: 978-1-4834-5170-1 (e)

Library of Congress Control Number: 2016907204

Lulu Publishing Services rev. date: 6/20/2016

This book is for Sally,

Who brought humor to life in art.

ACKNOWLEDGMENTS

No one writes a book without help from lots of people; for sure that's true for me and this book. Those who read earlier versions and liked it gave me the encouragement to complete it, and those who didn't like it, or didn't read all of it, gave me the encouragement to make it better so that they would!

So, without saying which category they were in, I acknowledge deep gratitude to my wife Judy, and friends Margo, Tom, Roger, Mike T., Gary, Judy E., Leigh, Jerry, Susie, Ann, Evy, Dan, Peter, Paul, Anne, Emmie, and especially Caroline. This list is of course not complete without mentioning Deuce, who listened to me talk through every story, and wagged his tail with approval or woofed to tell me to rework it until I got it right.

I am most thankful, however, to Michael G., who helped the most with this book. He made numerous suggestions, and proofread it multiple times. He challenged and argued with me over semicolons, commas, British versus American spellings, and choice of words. It was great fun working with Mike, and his help contributed tremendously to the final product.

Any failings or remaining errors, however, are mine alone.

Andrew Antijo

AUTHOR'S NOTE

This book is a fictional story about Deuce Clarence Jones' ancestors. Deuce Clarence Jones is a real dog, a Labrador retriever, and the *names* of his ancestors appearing in this book are real. Deuce's great-grandfather on his father's side was Bubbling Bedouine, a champion show dog. His great-grandmother was Tendercare Muskelunge Debbie; his grandfather was Tendercare Bubbling Buckeye, and his father was Skaggs' Westwood Gus. His grandmother on his mother's side was Ann Heuser, and his mother was Chocolate Molly II. But the stories about these dogs, their owners, the people involved with them, and what occurred in the places mentioned in the book are all fictitious.

A progenitor is a direct ancestor. A progenitor is also a model for something to come. The stories of Deuce's ancestors lead to the believability of the next book, which will be about him. If these dogs could do all the things they do in this book, there is no imagining what Deuce can do! *Book I – The Progenitors* sets the stage for the exploits of Deuce in subsequent books in the *Adventures of Deuce Clarence Jones* series.

PREFACE

Since this book may result in some readers thinking dogs can do pretty incredible, human-like things, I feel required to begin this preface with an apology to Cesar Millan. He has probably done more than any other single person to raise the awareness of people that dogs are not humans. Cesar has taught us that dogs don't think like humans, and are much happier if they are not expected to act like humans. He has made us aware of the problems we cause our dogs when we view and treat them as small furry humans. It is right to say that dogs are not humans. Cesar is absolutely correct.

Yet, what if a hundred, no, a thousand people passing by on the street were asked questions such as, can a baby read adult books at 18 months? Or, can a five-year-old compose a major symphony? Or, can a three-year-old solve complicated calculus equations, study physics at the university level, and speak a multitude of languages? I strongly believe the unanimous answer to each question would be "NO!"

In the human world there is that very occasional, extremely rare person we label a prodigy. A few examples (there aren't many) are William James Sidis, who could read at eighteen months, had written four books and was fluent in eight languages at age seven, gave a lecture at Harvard at nine and entered Harvard at eleven. Kim Ung-yong entered university as a physics student at the age of three, solving complicated calculus equations, composing poetry and speaking a multitude of languages, and getting his Ph.D. before most people graduate from high school. Howard Phillips Lovecraft learned to read at the age of two and was writing complex poetry by the age of six.

Carl Friedrich Gauss could sum 100 numbers in a couple of seconds in his elementary school classroom. Mozart learned to play the piano at the age of four, and composed his first pieces at five and at eight. Born in 1990, Gregory Smith could read at age two and had enrolled in university at age ten. He met with Bill Clinton and Mikhail Gorbachev, spoke in front of the UN and at age twelve was nominated for the Nobel Peace Prize. People like Galileo, Leonardo Da Vinci, or Sir Isaac Newton do not come along often, but they have.

One theory to explain extreme intelligence is that the brains of such people are more efficient. They pack more processing power into a small space. An analogy is to compare a computer in 1980 with a computer today. If man can expand the boundaries of technology to that degree, who is to say that on very rare occasions, nature does not also produce an extraordinary person who is many orders of magnitude above the rest of us in terms of abilities? Today, nanotechnology has the prospect of expanding the processing power of computers in a very small space to such a further degree that it cannot yet be comprehended. Cannot the same phenomenon occur on a random basis in nature, perhaps amplified by the chance of breeding? In addition, for reasons totally unknown, early stimulus being a possible guess, these unique people probably use *all* of their brain. They don't just coast along through life using the surface of their capabilities; they use all their capabilities to the fullest.

And if such rare capabilities can surface from time to time in the human race, is it not possible that the same phenomenon could occur in other species, perhaps in dogs?

What percentage of all humans have had such rare and unique capability? The absolute number of them throughout recorded history can be counted on both hands. The number of humans on the planet in March, 2012, was a bit over 7 billion. But the number of humans who ever lived on earth is about 107.6 billion. The odds of rare genius are incredibly high indeed.

Although Cesar Millan is absolutely correct; dogs are dogs, they are not humans, there have been a small number of dogs who appear at least to act as though they have intelligence—memory, reasoning ability, understanding, and judgment—approaching, or even the same as humans. This book is about a very few such dogs. Of that handful, one has those attributes in the extreme. Readers will generalize at their peril about any perception they have or judgment they might make concerning the dogs that appear in this book. They just won't apply to any dog you know (unless maybe it is your dog!). The dogs you will meet in this book are extraordinary. They are prodigies in the dog world. But the main dog in this series is a very special prodigy: Deuce Clarence Jones, truly the greatest dog ever!

Andrew Antijo

Book I - The Progenitors

CONTENTS

The Baltic Sea Area

Scale 1:10,000,000
Lambert Conformal Conic Projection,
standard parallels 55°N and 65°N

CIA Map Courtesy of University of Texas Libraries

CHAPTER 1

BUBBLING BEDOUINE

Can a person who is an oily, cheating scumbag have success at one of the most elegant, refined, genteel sports on the planet, a sport where one's reputation is more important that what is said or done? Well maybe, if he is also an ingratiating silver-tongued charmer. Groffudd Talfryn was both scumbag and charmer. His success depended on hiding his greasy character and misdeeds and succeeding at the latter. Travelling to other countries helped. Far away from home, no one knew the stories of his cheating on his wife, or of his defrauding and actually stealing from unsophisticated investors who trusted him to be the bright financial adviser he claimed to be, or of his now defunct home health care business which billed the Welsh government for fictitious services, or of his conviction for passing bad checks when he was in university (he got off with probation).

Groffudd was a con man with the proverbial silver tongue. He had used it in many prior schemes to talk people into giving him money under false pretenses. He would often approach a stranger with some story in order to make a quick buck. These petty scams were like a game to Groffudd; it was exciting whenever he succeeded in conning someone. His mark was usually completely taken in, while anyone else watching and listening but not emotionally involved was often intrigued and then repulsed by what he was hearing.

His current scheme was much bigger than a petty scam. It was to marry his avocation of raising Labrador retrievers with the other two things he was good at: charming and cheating. He did have an absolutely fabulous dog, and he was an experienced dog trainer. His aim was to have his dog, Dylan, become the international champion Labrador retriever. Dylan would then be a veritable money machine for his master. The stud fees for an international champion dog could be as high as ten thousand euros or more. If Dylan could garner the international champion title he would make Groffudd a very wealthy man.

Groffudd had planned since Dylan was born for him to be a show dog. Dylan was as black as anthracite from the Welsh hills. His full name, Dylan Du Hyrwyddwr, meant "Great Flowing Black Champion" in Welsh. Groffudd knew how to train dogs and had worked ceaselessly to enhance Dylan's appearance and demeanor as a conformance show dog. Dylan had daily training sessions to refine how he should present himself at shows. He was taught to stand with his head and chest forward, back legs back, and tail tilted upward; to present the best profile when he sat, to hold his pose while he was examined by the judge, and, most importantly, how to move as his handler led him around the ring for the judge and the audience to see how he carried himself. The work and effort showed and objectively, Dylan really was a great show dog.

To become a champion show dog, a dog must first win points towards the designation. Dylan had won many points and awards in conformance shows, which are supposed to determine the best representative of the breed. Dogs are judged as to how well they conform to a set of standards adopted by the national clubs. The standards for Labrador retrievers are over three pages long. Objective physical standards govern size, proportion, and substance, meaning that the dog is neither light and weedy in appearance or cloddy and lumbering. However, there are also standards that are much less objective, governing movement and temperament. Dylan had won the champion designation in several smaller shows in Wales and the country champion designation in Latvia and Bulgaria. What no one knew, however, except Groffudd and the judges at those two later shows, was that Groffudd had paid them to throw the title to Dylan.

The World Global Dog Show, which selected the international champion for each breed, was seventeen years old and conducted dog shows annually, each year in a different country. It was bigger and longer than Crufts held in Birmingham, England, or the Westminster Kennel Club Dog Show held at Madison Square Garden in New York. It had attracted a huge number of entrants in its first year. The next year, to make it more manageable, entry was limited to dogs who had already won at least one champion designation in any dog show. There were still more qualified applicants than could easily be accommodated. Time limits for applying were tried next, and then a first-apply, first-admitted policy with a cut-off limit for each breed was tried. However, the show had become so popular that many champion show dogs were denied entry. So for the 1998 World Global Dog Show in Helsinki, Finland, the organizers had announced it would be restricted to dogs who had won at least one *country* champion designation. That meant that a champion designation in a show that did not purport to select the champion for an entire country did not qualify the dog for the World Global show; only those that had already been judged the best dog in a country dog show were qualified. But there was no requirement that a dog had to actually reside in the country for which it won a country title.

That's why Groffudd had taken Dylan to the country shows in Latvia and Bulgaria. They were smaller shows, where he thought Dylan had a good chance of winning a country champion title. But he was also very much aware that the selection of a champion had a large subjective element. At each succeeding level of competition, more of the dogs clearly met all the objective standards for judging. And in the country shows, and really in all shows where entry was restricted, practically all the dogs met the objective standards for their breed. So the selection of the champion became more and more subjective as a dog moved up to those shows. Groffudd hadn't wanted to take any chances, which is why he had paid a bribe to each judge in the Latvia and Bulgaria country shows to assure Dylan would have a country champion title and thereby qualify for the World Global Dog Show, which selected the international champions.

After traveling most of the day from their home in Llanelli, Wales, Groffudd and Dylan checked into the Hilton Helsinki Kalastajatorppa in Helsinki, Finland. They were repeat customers, as they had stayed there before when they went to dog shows in Helsinki. The hotel was one of the few dog-friendly hotels close to the convention center, where all the big dog shows in Helsinki were held. The 1998 World Global Dog Show was to begin the next day.

Since every dog competing at the World Global Dog Show was a champion in some country, and because it was the biggest show of all, the element of subjectivity in picking the best of the breeds would be higher than in any other show. And since the name of the judge for each event would not be announced until judging began, one would think that it would be difficult to bribe any judge at that show. However, Groffudd knew differently. Judges were picked by the national associations and had to demonstrate expert knowledge of the breed. Not many judges were qualified to judge more than one breed, and they traveled around to all of the dog shows.

Groffudd knew many of the prominent judges for Labrador retrievers. He had made it a point to socialize with most of them, buying dinners before dog shows and entertaining each—always individually—at every opportunity. It had been a simple process of elimination to find out who would be the judge of the Labrador retrievers at the World Global Dog Show. Groffudd simply called each of the prominent Labrador retriever judges in turn and invited him to dinner at an expensive restaurant the night before the show. The ones who declined said they could not accept, because they would not be there. So the one who accepted, Judge Robbison Rawley, was obviously going to judge the Labrador retrievers at the Global Dog Show.

Groffudd's dinner with Robbison Rawley was at the Cuisinier & Sommelier at 48 Huvilakatu, not far from Groffudd's hotel, and clearly the best restaurant in Helsinki. Groffudd had arranged for them to be seated in a booth at the back of the restaurant. They joked with the sommelier and were entertained by his anecdotes about his favorite wineries. The chef came to their booth and served vegetables he had picked from his own garden.

As they enjoyed a four-course meal, not a word was said by either of them about the dog show the next day. But in the course of the conversation, after a number of scotch-and-sodas, Judge Rawley let slip that his wife had divorced him and pretty much had taken him to the cleaners. She had hired a detective who found out about the lengthy affair he had had with a woman twenty years his junior who was his wife's personal trainer. His wife was red-hot furious. The personal trainer just got fired, but Judge Rawley lost almost three-fourths of his fortune—half went to his wife, and about a fourth went to the attorneys. That gave Groffudd the opening he had been looking for, but he waited until the next day to use it.

The next morning, Groffudd took Dylan to the Helsinki convention center for the start of the World Global Dog Show. Dylan had to stay in a cage in an area on the main floor of the large building with all the other Labrador retrievers. Groffudd was just closing the gate on Dylan's cage when he spotted Judge Rawley.

"Hey Judge!" he called out. "Can I see you a moment?"

Judge Rawley felt just a bit annoyed since he didn't want to be seen talking to an owner before the judging, but still he approached Groffudd.

Groffudd said, "I know you shouldn't see my dog before the show. Let's move over here a bit."

Relieved, Judge Rawley followed him. They stopped in front of the cage of another dog.

Groffudd went on, "I remember you telling me you would like to get another dog since you lost your last one. You remember my black Lab, Dylan. One of his litters will be born in about three weeks. These will be great pups. I get the pick of the litter. I know you need a new dog and I want to give it to you."

Judge Rawley hadn't lost a dog, hadn't mentioned he wanted a dog, and wasn't looking for a dog. But he immediately knew what Groffudd was offering. This had nothing to do with him getting a dog. It was all about how much Groffudd would pay him to throw the championship to Dylan. Rawley knew that a pup fathered by Dylan would be valuable, and that it would be immensely more valuable if Dylan was named the international champion. Groffudd was offering him what an international champion's pup was worth. He thought a moment, about how much he needed the money.

Then he said to Groffudd, "You know that any dog that wins has to be absolutely perfect in his poses and so forth."

Groffudd said, "I'm giving you the pup, no matter what happens in this dog show. This show has nothing to do with it."

Which is the way they would both portray it if anyone found out.

It so happened that Bubbling Bedouine, the Finnish national champion Labrador retriever, was in the cage next to where both men were talking. Bubbling heard the word "Dylan" and his ears perked up. He had competed against Dylan in several previous shows and knew Groffudd was his owner. He listened to the quiet, intense tone of the conversation. Something did not seem right. He didn't know what was going on, but it made him nervous. Bubbling was a smart dog but of course there is no way of knowing if he understood what he overheard. However, his muscles tightened, his head raised, and his heightened alertness indicated that he clearly sensed that Groffudd was up to something and it wasn't good. Then he saw Judge Rawley nod his head and the men parted. Body language is more important to a dog than any other form of communication. Bubbling knew that some kind of agreement had been made, and that it involved Dylan.

Bubbling had competed against Dylan and didn't like him. In both temperament and demeanor Bubbling was very friendly, whereas Dylan was aloof. If a dog could have a superiority complex, that was Dylan. Bubbling thought he was stuck up and a boor. Both of them were very competitive, but Bubbling was competitive without being arrogant, like Dylan was.

While Bubbling was also a show dog, he had a more relaxed life. His owner was Madagascar (Maddy) Modulessi, whose main job was being a liquor distributor. Unlike Groffudd, Maddy didn't spend as much time training his dog or taking him around to all the dog shows. His hobby was to breed chocolate Labrador retrievers and he was good at it. But his primary activity was selling booze to bars. So Bubbling didn't get the extreme refinement in training that Dylan did. Because of fewer shows and less intense training, Bubbling had fewer awards than Dylan.

Nevertheless, Bubbling Bedouine was the Finnish national champion Labrador retriever, and a fantastic dog. He had a wonderful chocolate caramel colored coat that women and girls would die to run their fingers through. He won his first champion award in his first year, which was expected of him. It was expected of him because his father, and his grandfather, and his great grandfather, *and* his mother, and her father, and his father, were all champions. Sixteen of his ancestors were champions. Most of them won their championships in England. So it was no surprise that Bubbling Bedouine also became a champion.

Bubbling's strength was his personality. He liked to show off, in a good way. Also, his movements were fluid. He was like grace on ice. But he hadn't mastered his stand poses quite to the extent as Dylan had. He was good, but there was a doubt. Was he good enough to beat Dylan? Maybe, but maybe not. And the tone of Groffudd's conversation he had overheard made him nervous. Bubbling knew a big show was about to happen and wanted to win. So he did something he would later regret. Bubbling knew Dylan had a weakness for just about any female show dog. He thought Dylan would have trouble holding a pose if he could be distracted, and Bubbling Bedouine thought he knew how to distract him.

When the competition began that afternoon by the luck of the draw Dylan was called first, before Bubbling, which gave him his chance. Bubbling was waiting in the warm up area and he moved close to the prettiest female of the group that was waiting for its turn on the stage. That was Dacy Delacy Delecatacey. Dacy Delacy looked like a treat to Bubbling, and if he could hardly resist her allure and temptation, he knew Dylan would never be able to hold the critical stand pose needed to garner the champion title if he wanted to look at Dacy Delacy. Bubbling thought he knew just how to make that happen.

Dylan was absolutely perfect when he was examined by Judge Rawley, and in his prance around the ring, and his sit pose. But then thirty seconds or so after Dylan began his "stand" pose, which he had to hold for two minutes—his final pose which would garner him the championship, for sure! —Bubbling nipped Dacy Delacy on the butt. Everyone's eyes were on Dylan, so no one saw the nip. But Dacy Delacy sure felt it. She gave a short high pitched shriek; high pitched enough that the judge didn't hear it. But Dylan did, and at that moment broke his pose to turn to look at Dacy Delacy Delecatacey. And in a world where a dog has to be absolutely perfect to be the international champion, Dylan failed.

When it was his turn, Bubbling Bedouine did not fail. He did every sit pose perfectly, and his movement around the ring with grace and fluid motion, and his stand pose with studied perfection. And all the while, he conveyed a sense of joy in what he was doing. It was not a task, a learned move, a requirement. There was a sparkle in his eyes, a seeming smile on his face. It was, *Wow,* this is great! This is fun! Bubbling Bedouine connected with the crowd. They were on their feet applauding! Judge Rawley hesitated for a moment. He wanted to award the champion title to Dylan but he knew he couldn't. The planned "fix" would be too obvious. Judge Rawley made the only decision he could make. His announcement blared over the loudspeakers to every corner of the great exhibit hall in the Helsinki convention center, which was packed to capacity. "Bubbling Bedouine is the new International Champion Labrador Retriever!"

Groffudd and Dylan returned to Llanelli that evening. Groffudd was furious with Dylan, who could not understand why his owner was so angry. Groffudd didn't know that Bubbling Bedouine had caused Dylan to break his pose, which caused him to lose the championship. He probably would have been even madder—but not at Dylan—if he knew what had happened. But he didn't, and so Dylan took the brunt of his wrath.

The day after the show ended, Bubbling sat on a large pallograniitti rock in front of Maddy's house on Kymintie Street in Helsinki and watched people as they passed by. He thought about the show, and the memory of what he had done now troubled him. He thought he really needn't have nipped Dacy Delacy Delecatacey on the butt to win. But he had and it detracted from the joy of his performance at the dog show. He knew he would carry with him the rest of his life a blot on the memory of his championship. It was a stain on his accomplishment that only he (and obviously, Dacy) knew about, but that didn't matter. He knew that he hadn't played 100% fair, even though a champion is supposed to be able to withstand and ignore any and all distractions. He didn't know that Groffudd hadn't played fair either. And so he didn't think about whether that would have made any difference.

Since he was now the international champion, Bubbling got constant attention. Maddy made sure he got the best food, care and companionship, and training to improve his skills. He had two handlers who went with him (one at a time, of course) throughout the day, so he was never alone. He got to spend time with Dacy Delacy Delecatacey, and many others like her. Maddy was paid for him to do so, so it was not an option. Bubbling was a gigolo, some would say. He didn't get to choose, he was expected to perform with every female presented to him, and while he didn't get paid, Maddy did. After a while, however, this parade of females got to be boring for Bubbling Bedouine. It was a chore, a job. There was no thrill of the chase, never any doubt as to his conquest, *no resistance*! What romance or fun is it if you always win?

Not everything else about being the international champion was all that great, either. Bubbling couldn't run with any other males, because his handlers didn't want to take any chance he might get in a fight and get hurt. He wasn't allowed to go exploring on his own, and he quickly became bored with the same old places the handlers took him. He did get to go to a show every other month or so, where he would go through all the moves and poses that made him the international champion. And he would always do it perfectly, with an attitude of fun and joy that absolutely captivated the crowd. In a word, he personified his first name—he was "bubbling" with personality. And in every show after he won the international champion designation, he always won first place. No other competitor was even close. He enjoyed these shows, and the more the crowds responded to him, the more he was energized by them, and the better his performance became. But the routine of the shows never changed.

Bubbling Bedouine did get to see at least from a distance, some other females who had not been brought to him. For reasons he did not fathom he was not allowed near them. The reason was not that difficult to understand but it never occurred to Bubbling. It was because his coat was chocolate, and these females were black. And the blackest of them all and the best looking, by far, without any doubt, was Tendercare Muskelunge Debbie. Debbie was not just any color black, but anthracite black, like Dylan Du Hyrwyddwr. Black so black that it doesn't absorb light, it reflects it!

Debbie conveyed an allure, a softness, a sense of vulnerability that captivated every male that saw her. There was a certain tenderness about her that made Bubbling's heart seem to melt. But the attribute that absolutely drove him mad, almost insane with desire, was her smell. Debbie exuded a scent, a musky scent that practically caused Bubbling to lunge for Debbie from across the large exhibit hall. Whoever had named her had done so appropriately.

Tendercare Muskelunge Debbie was a champion in her own right, which meant that she was guarded around the clock, fenced off from all males. She was allowed only females as companions, and at the right time, would mate only with a black champion male. However, since Bubbling Bedouine had won the international championship, there was no black international champion male Labrador retriever. Debbie's owner decided that when the time came, she would mate with Dylan Du Hyrwyddwr, who after all did have country champion awards. In addition to outstanding physique, both Debbie and Dylan had the best black color. Their offspring were expected to have all of the outstanding attributes of both parents, particularly their shining black color.

All of the top dogs were at the next country dog show in Helsinki. This was the largest and most famous annual show in Finland and it attracted entrants from all over Europe. The facility used to host this show was again the Helsinki convention center, where Bubbling Bedouine had won his international champion title the year before. Each different breed of dogs was kept in its own area for the duration of the show and some of the breeds were even kept in separate buildings while they were waiting their turn to compete. The show lasted three days, and cages had been brought in for all the dogs. The Labrador retrievers were the most popular, so they were kept in the Great Exhibit Hall in the convention center itself. This was because visitors to the show always wanted to look at them, even when they were not on the stage competing. Each dog had a cage; the males were on one side of the room, and the females on the other. Bubbling and Dylan were there with the other males, and by chance their cages were next to each other. On the other side of the room, Dacy Delacy Delecatacey and Tendercare Muskelunge Debbie were expected to be present along with the other top female Labrador retrievers.

Bubbling had been in his cage for two hours on the morning of the first day of the show and he was bored. He was waiting his turn to compete in the preliminaries, which for the Labradors would occur early that afternoon. He even got tired of smiling and wagging his tail at the parade of visitors who endlessly passed by his cage, one after the other, remarking, "Oh, what a good looking dog." "Oh, what a good looking dog." "Oh, what a good looking dog." "Oh, what a good looking dog."

Bubbling thought to himself, goodness, can't these people come up with anything different to say? What do they expect to see, a cat? You would think that at least one of them would say, oh, what a handsome dog, or that's a great looking dog. Or, I like this dog. They sounded like a broken record, and Bubbling tried to tune them out and take a nap.

Just then, however, some of the females who were going to compete in the preliminaries later in the afternoon were brought into the room. They passed within twenty feet of Bubbling's cage, and he awoke from his half sleep. He first saw Dacy Delacy Delecatacey, and then he smelled Tendercare Muskelunge Debbie. He jumped to his feet and pressed against the wire mesh of his cage. He caught sight of her and then she was gone, across the room where her handler put her in her own cage. Bubbling stood looking after her, long after she disappeared from his sight. Her lingering smell tormented him, and he told himself that one way or another he would find a way to be with her. But he also knew this was not the time. He sighed and slumped to the floor, knowing he could not get out of the cage.

Dylan, in the next cage, also smelled Tendercare Muskelunge Debbie when she passed by the cages with the male Labrador retrievers. Dylan was not tormented by her smell as was Bubbling; he reacted with excitement and anticipation. He knew she was his. Groffudd had told him that a deal had been made, and that Debbie was promised to him. He only had to wait for the right time. That time could not come too soon, but Dylan could wait with the confidence of knowing he would soon be with her. He too lay down in his cage but unlike Bubbling, who was fretting with anxiety and uncertainty in the cage next to him, Dylan was relaxed and at peace with himself.

The afternoon preliminaries were uneventful for the top rated show dogs like Bubbling and Dylan. Each of them effortlessly performed all of the required routines, moves and poses. Bubbling as usual got more applause from the crowd, but each easily advanced to the next and final round, scheduled for the next day. Then it was back to the Labrador area, and a walk outside with a handler. After a brisk hour long exercise walk, each returned to the exhibit hall area for dinner and a drink.

The routine for Bubbling included a short night walk several hours after dinner, followed by a good brushing from his handler, and then, as a final step, cleaning his teeth with enzymatic toothpaste and a toothbrush. Bubbling liked this last step; it was fun to have his teeth brushed and it was also good for his appearance and his smile. His teeth looked like polished ivory. Because this routine usually started after 9:00 pm, it was at the least desirable time for the handlers, and so it generally, as it did that night, fell to the handler with the least seniority. That was Eustis Izzielustus, who was also the least experienced handler.

Bubbling knew Eustis and thought he was a fool. Eustis was always talking about how much he knew about dogs, and bragging that he was the caretaker for the international champion. In fact, Eustis didn't know much about dogs at all. He didn't know dog language, and he certainly didn't know how to talk to them. He didn't even understand their different barks and sounds. Worse, he didn't know how to read dog body language, which for anyone who works with dogs is absolutely essential, at a minimum.

On the walk that night, Bubbling thought of a plan to get free so he could find Tendercare Debbie. He was so excited he couldn't contain his nervous energy. But Eustis was oblivious to Bubbling's emotional energy. Eustis was just bumbling along, anxious to get through with this last chore and not paying any attention at all to his charge. When they returned to the cage area, Eustis, with the reluctant air of someone with no enthusiasm for his job got ready to brush Bubbling's coat and brush his teeth. He dropped the leash and got the dog brush, toothbrush and toothpaste out of the travelling box next to Bubbling's cage. Then he unfastened Bubbling's collar so he could start brushing his neck. The instant the collar was off Bubbling whirled around and bumped his head into Eustis' midriff, knocking him backward. Bubbling then took off running.

As Bubbling took off, Eustis fell backward, directly into a bucket full of water that was used to clean mud off of dogs' feet. This was a big bucket, and his rump went right into it. Eustis was wedged in the bucket of water with his hands and feet in the air. He wildly thrust his upper body from side to side trying to get out, tipping the bucket over in the process. Now all of his pants were wet from the spilled water. Eustis jumped up screaming for Bubbling, who was nowhere to be seen. He reached for his back pocket, pulled out a radio alarm that all of the handlers carried, and frantically pushed the button that would send an alarm and summon help. But nothing happened—the alarm had gone directly into the bucket of water and shorted out. It was useless. A wave of panic engulfed Eustis, but he caught himself and then yelled to all the other handlers he could see in the area to help him find Bubbling Bedouine. In less than a minute, three men, Clerfus, Zegger, and Wisfusen were running with Eustis for the main door to the Great Hall to help find the escaping dog.

After knocking Eustis into the bucket, Bubbling Bedouine had run for that door. It was a heavy door, but not locked, and he pushed it open enough to get through. The Great Hall of the convention center is on the north side of the city of Helsinki, in a busy area. The main door is on the southeast corner of the building, facing Ratamestarinkatu Street. A long row of dense bushes lines the street opposite this side of the building. Bubbling ducked down behind these bushes and lay still. With his chocolate coat, he was practically invisible in the dark. From that point he watched Eustis and the other handlers run out the door into the street. They stopped, not knowing which way to go. After an excited few moments of conversation, they split up, each going a separate direction. Eustis went south on Ratamestarinkatu, Clerfus went north toward the Banmastargatan, Zegger went east on Bromsargatan, and Wisfusen proceeded west on Jarnvagsmannagatan toward the main thoroughfare, Bangardsvgen Boulevard.

After about twenty unsuccessful minutes of running and calling for Bubbling, each realized the futility of trying to find a chocolate dog in the dark. At about the same time, all four of them gave up and started to walk back to the convention center. At this point, Eustis' heart was palpitating with fear; he could hardly walk and felt like he was about to throw up. He was sure to get fired from his job, and he was very much afraid.

Tendercare Muskelunge Debbie had left the Great Hall with her handler about twenty minutes before Bubbling Bedouine bumped Eustis into the bucket of water. She enjoyed her walk through the side streets around the convention center in the cool night air. It had been an uneventful walk and her handler, a young lady named Cecilia, had enjoyed it as much as Debbie. As they approached the Great Hall Debbie stiffened, scenting Bubbling Bedouine behind the row of bushes. Cecilia had her mind on getting back to the building, hoping to run into Wisfusen. She had been trying to catch his eye all that day. She wasn't paying much attention to her dog and didn't notice the tenseness in Debbie's body. Bubbling had sensed Debbie before she sensed him. Had anyone been watching him—impossible in the dark—they would have seen his muscles tense as he waited. At just the moment before Cecilia could notice him, but also when the distance he would have to run to Debbie was the least, he sprang from behind the bushes and in a split second was beside Debbie, with her leash in his mouth. He tried to bite through it but it had a steel wire inside the leather leash and he could not break it. Cecilia whirled around as Bubbling pulled on the leash and started yelling and kicking at him. Bubbling quickly knew he could not bite through the leash, so he yanked to pull it away from Cecilia. He pulled so quickly and with such force that it went right out of her hands.

Bubbling barked to Debbie, "Come on!"

Both dogs took off down Ratamestarinkatu Street, as fast as they could go, with Cecilia in pursuit. Ratamestarinkatu Street turned into a hilly area a half mile or so from the convention center. There were a number of culverts under the street for storm water to drain through where the street crossed over ravines. Bubbling Bedouine knew this street well, and when it descended into one of these ravines he and Debbie ran to the north side of the street and down the slope to the entrance of the first culvert. They had left Cecilia far behind, frantically shouting for Debbie, as Eustis Izzielustus had just as ineffectively shouted for Bubbling. They had to crouch a bit as they entered the culvert and with Bubbling leading the way, with Debbie's leash still in his mouth, they went as fast as they could through the culvert. They came out on the other side in a deserted wooded area.

At that point, Bubbling felt a wave of relief sweep over him. He slowed to a walk and his heart stopped racing. He looked at Debbie who was a step behind him, looking expectantly back at him. Bubbling realized he still had her leash in his mouth and stopped. He let her know he had to do something about that. She lay on the ground, and Bubbling, with his head next to hers, bit with his front teeth into her collar. A few gnashes back and forth with his teeth separated the layers of the leather collar and it parted. Unlike the leash, the collar did not have a steel wire in it. Debbie was free! Bubbling and Debbie ran on through the dense woods until they came upon a small opening under a large pine. The tree's branches reached the ground all around this opening, which made the space under the tree look like a cave. Bubbling and Debbie entered the cave and lay down on the deep soft pine needles, panting to recover after their run from the convention center.

Now, Bubbling didn't know (and if he did, wouldn't have cared) that Maddy, his owner, was trying to breed the best chocolate Labrador retrievers. Or that Debbie's owner was trying to breed the best black Labs. Nor did he know how difficult that is.

Their owners didn't understand it either. Sometimes when they bred two black Labrador retrievers, the result often was a litter of pups with all three colors. It was even more confusing if Labs of two different colors were bred. The owners didn't know a geneticist who had studied the matter. If they had found such an expert, the conversation might have gone as follows:

"How the *%#* did I get a chocolate pup from two blacks?

"Well, the pup got a recessive color gene from each black parent, and at least one dominant epistatic gene from one of the parents."

"What does that mean?"

"Well, the dominant color gene is for black, and the recessive color gene is for chocolate. Your chocolate pup has a recessive color gene from each parent. And also at least one dominant epistatic gene, from either parent, in order for the color to be in the dog's coat. Yellow Labs have two recessive epistatic genes."

"Don't talk to me in gobbledygook! You're using words I don't know. Explain that in plain English!"

"Didn't you take high school biology? The pup had to get two recessive color genes and at least one gene that causes the color to be deposited in the dog's fur. That's called an epistatic gene."

"Forget that I asked you. You're obnubilating the whole thing!"

"Are you calling me names now? Go figure it out for yourself."

Unknown to either of their owners, because genotyping of dogs was not very common (and had not been done for these two dogs), Bubbling carried two recessive genes for color, and two dominant epistatic genes. Debbie carried one dominant and one recessive color gene, and two dominant epistatic genes. Although their owners didn't know it, that meant that if these two dogs were bred, none of their puppies would be yellow, and it would be a coin toss as to whether any individual puppy would be black or chocolate. Their genotypes—the genetic makeup of the two Labrador retrievers, and chance, explain why Bubbling's tryst with Debbie would cause so much anger and consternation exactly 63 days hence.

Early the next morning Bubbling and Debbie returned to the convention center. The Best of Show would be judged later that day, and Bubbling wanted to win. Even though they were the most popular breed, no Labrador retriever had previously ever won Best of Show, in *any* dog show. So if Bubbling could win Best of Show in addition to breed specific awards, it would be huge. Both dogs slipped in through the main door as the dog handlers were going about their business, prior to opening the center to the public. No one seemed to notice as Bubbling went to his cage. The door was ajar and he entered and lay down. He lay there and tried to visualize how it would feel to be on the top platform and receive the highest award of the entire competition.

Debbie was unnoticed until she got to within about 50 feet of her cage, when she was spotted by Cecilia. Cecilia was so overjoyed to see Debbie that she couldn't be angry. She rushed to her and threw her arms around Debbie, who was madly wagging her tail. But then as she was leading Debbie to her cage, Cecilia was struck by the dilemma she now faced. Unlike Eustis, who had called for help after Bubbling knocked him into the pail of water when he escaped, Cecilia had run after Debbie herself. She had not yet told anyone about Debbie's absence. Bubbling's escape was the talk of all the handlers and word had just gotten out that Eustis was fired because of it. Cecilia was now afraid the same would happen to her. She shut the door on Debbie's cage and walked away in a quandary. Her mind churned over whether she should tell Debbie's owner what had happened the previous night. Finally, she decided to take her chances and not talk about it.

CHAPTER 2

BUCKEY

The show at the convention center continued without incident. The escapade of the night before was quickly forgotten, as everyone focused on the competition. Bubbling won another champion award for best Labrador retriever, and then won the award for best of the sporting group, which includes pointers, retrievers, setters and spaniels. But a Pekingese named "Fluffy" won Best of Show. Bubbling couldn't believe it! He was the best of the most popular breed of all dogs, and he got beat by a dog that looked like a small mop. Debbie also took first in her class. Dylan again came in second to Bubbling as the best Labrador, which had become the pattern at show after show when they both competed. At the end of the show, all the dogs were taken to their home or kennel, to get on with their lives. For most of them, it was continuing to train to be able to compete better in the next show. Such is the life of a show dog.

But for Debbie, it was a special time. The week after the show was the time she would mate with Dylan. She probably wouldn't have picked Dylan if she had had a choice; she didn't much care for his personality. He was stilted, and had a big ego. His striking poses and prances in the dog ring had won him many awards, but to those who watched him closely, he was cold and aloof, with his nose in the air. Nevertheless, a dog must do what a dog must do. Dylan was brought to Debbie's kennel, and the handlers then left them alone.

A number of weeks went by. Debbie enjoyed this time. She didn't have to train, and Cecilia gave her all the food she wanted. She got to go on short walks twice a day, and lie out in the sun the rest of the time. After about eight weeks Debbie began feeling restless and irritable. She didn't respond well to Cecilia's effort to interest her in food, toys, walks, affection, or much of anything. After a couple of days of this, she began to collect all sorts of stray pieces of cloth, old towels, and even an old blanket that had been left out on top of a chest of drawers that was in the garage near her kennel. She did this surreptitiously, when Cecilia wasn't around, and used these items to make a soft nest in the back of her kennel.

The next morning when Cecilia came to the kennel she heard something she had not heard for a long while. Soft, gentle squealing sounds came from the kennel. Cecilia looked through the door into the dark kennel. Since she was in front of the door, she couldn't see anything. She moved to one side, letting the light enter, and then she saw what had happened. First, one small pup poked his head up, his eyes tightly shut and unseeing. Then she saw another, and then another, and when she had counted them all there were eight newborn pups. Debbie, a calm, proud mother, was licking them and cleaning them up for the first time, to introduce them to the world.

Cecilia ran from the kennel to the big house where Alfonso Attataccus, Debbie's owner, lived with his wife Mariana and their six children. Cecilia ran into the house yelling "Debbie had her pups! Debbie had her pups! Come and see them! I think there are eight pups!" Alfonso and Mariana with three of the children following rushed down the stairs through the hallway to the great room where Cecilia had entered.

"Are you sure?" asked Alfonso.

"Yes, yes, come and see," Cecilia replied.

Mariana began pulling on her coat and helping the children to get theirs. Tymoco, the oldest, and his sister, Verviana, were out the door first, followed by Meganosa, Feopatifus, Cynadita, and Lapaidacus, the youngest, bringing up the rear. They all ran for the kennel, which was in the back of the big garage a hundred or so feet behind the house.

They were almost to the garage when Alfonso thought to himself, how can this be? It's almost a week early!

Alfonso and Mariana had owned many champion dogs. They were well known breeders, and while they truly liked dogs, breeding had become a business for them, which supplemented Alfonso's not insubstantial income as an orthodontist in a large practice with three other orthodontists. Alfonso was the managing partner of the practice. Even though he made a lot of money from his main business, he and Mariana also spent a lot of money, on themselves, their six children, and on travelling, mostly throughout southern Europe and the Mediterranean. They liked to get out of the cold Finnish winters as much as possible. That was one reason they had hired Cecilia to take care of the dogs, so they could travel as they wished. So while the champion dog breeding business was not their main source of livelihood, it was nevertheless important, and Alfonso was counting on the sale of Debbie's pups to finance their next trip to the Greek Islands. He had even bought the airplane tickets for the family, and planned to use money from the sale of the pups for hotel rooms (the family needed three rooms to accommodate all of them) and food for two weeks in Greece.

When Alfonso saw Debbie and the pups, he was very worried. He then said what he was thinking, "How can this be? It's only been 58 days, and it should be 63 days."

"You're right, they're early," replied Mariana.

Both of them knew the gestation period for a mother dog is 63 days. They had not expected Debbie's pups to be born until five days later. Just like Cecilia, Alfonso couldn't see very well into the dark kennel. Tymoco and Verviana were crowding in front of the door to the kennel, making it even more difficult to see in, and the other children were crying and pushing to get a look through the door.

Alfonso was annoyed and anxious. "Everybody get back; we'll all get a look. We all have to take turns."

Mariana took Tymoco's arm and pulled him back, saying, "Stand aside and let daddy look in first."

The light streamed into the kennel as the family moved back. Alfonso got his first good look at the pups. He counted them as had Cecilia; eight pups. Then it hit him: these pups were not black, they were *all chocolate*!

Alfonso screamed, "Some other dog got to Debbie, these are not Dylan's pups. They can't be! How the heck did this happen?! Who did this?"

Mariana and the children were silent. Mariana knew how much money they would lose by not being able to sell eight pups from champion parents. She had a fleeting thought of losing their upcoming vacation to the Greek Islands.

Then she called, "Cecilia, do you know anything about this?"

Cecilia had not focused on the fact that the pups were chocolate, not black. Now she did. Alfonso was beginning to think back, to remember what was going on before he arranged for Dylan to mate with Debbie. Cecilia's mind was racing, a step ahead of his. It flashed through her head, should she now tell him Debbie had escaped from the convention center Great Hall during the last show, and was gone for a night? For whatever reason she would not know, other than her parents had instilled in her the value of honesty, she quickly decided to tell what had happened, (well, almost).

She told them, "On the second night of the dog show, Debbie got out of the hall. So did Bubbling Bedouine. Eustis and I and several of the others chased them. They were gone for a few hours, but we got them back and I didn't think anything happened. So I didn't think it was important to mention it earlier."

Alfonso obviously knew all about Bubbling Bedouine. Everyone in the dog world did. He would have had Bubbling mate with Debbie himself, if Bubbling had been a black Labrador, instead of a chocolate. He thought it amazing that all eight pups were chocolate. Maybe if Bubbling Bedouine *was* the father of these pups, he would not lose so much money after all.

Alfonso arranged for a DNA test of the pups. He called Bubbling's owner, Madagascar Modulessi, and got permission to get DNA from Bubbling. He got the results of the DNA test the next day. Sure enough,

Bubbling Bedouine was the father of these pups. Alfonso put an ad in the *Helsinki Times Express* announcing the offering of seven champion bred Labrador retriever pups. The eighth went to Bubbling's owner, Maddy, who got first pick of the pups in payment for Bubbling being the father of the litter. The seven pups were all spoken for on the first day the ad ran, and Alfonso made more money that he had expected to make from the litter had it been sired by Dylan.

Alfonso finally had time to think about what to do about Cecilia not telling him immediately that Debbie had escaped. Since everything had turned out better than he first expected, he was in a good mood. He gave Cecilia only a reprimand and a warning to immediately contact him if anything like that were to happen again.

Maddy Modulessi didn't really want Debbie's pup. Like Alfonso, who was trying to breed only the best black Labradors, he was trying to breed the best chocolate Labradors. Both of them wanted the purest color, the best of the best black (or chocolate) for their dogs. Alfonso didn't want any coffee colored black Labrador, and Maddy didn't want any possible shades of black in his chocolate Labradors. The purchasers of the seven pups that Alfonso sold didn't seem to be so sophisticated, and weren't buying the pups for breeding anyway. They were buying them so they could tell their friends that their dog was the son (or daughter) of Bubbling Bedouine! For most of them, purchasing one of these pups was as much an ego trip as it was getting a good dog. So they either didn't know or care that much about purity of color, or maybe they got snookered. Maddy advertised the pup he got—the pick of the litter—in the *Helsinki Times Express*, as Alfonso had done. But he also put an ad in the *International Dog Breeders Journal*, and on the internet on the Best of Dog Breeds website. And he asked a lot more money for the pup than had Alfonso. After all he did have the pick of the litter, and this pup was a male.

In Shaker Heights, just outside of Cleveland, Ohio in the United States, Ralph Rapaski sat down in his scarlet and gray arm chair (it had a scarlet seat and gray arms) in the dining nook off of the kitchen to his house. That was where he sat after he got up every morning, to have a cup of coffee and read the morning newspaper, *The Cleveland Plain Dealer*. The entire kitchen was scarlet and gray like the chair; the walls were scarlet and the ceiling was gray. The top of the back of the chair he sat in had the inscription "OHIO STATE." A moment later, Ralph's wife, Annabella, brought him his coffee—with a splash of cream in it—in a white cup with a scarlet ring around the top and a gray ring around the bottom. It was inscribed "OHIO STATE" on one side, and "GO BUCKS!" on the other side. Ralph, as you might guess, was a rabid Ohio State fan, and less enthusiastic neighbors and friends regarded him as practically unbearable since that year the Ohio State Buckeyes were undefeated after their first ten games. Ralph also had to have just enough cream in his coffee, to give it a "chocolate" like look. Ralph was fanatical about all of his interests, and after Ohio State his next most fanatical interest was chocolate Labrador retrievers. So obviously, he couldn't drink black coffee.

After she brought Ralph his coffee, Annabella dumped a stack of letters and magazines in front of Ralph, saying, "Ralphie," (this slightly annoyed him, but he never asked her not to call him that) "here's yesterday's mail. You didn't go through it and there may be some bills or stuff in it you should see."

Ralph was a bit irritated, since he was just into his paper and only partly through the sports section, which he was scanning for any possible story about Ohio State football. He didn't find any other than the one on the first page of that section, which he read. Then he put down the paper, picked up the mail, and looked through it. Half way through the stack, he came to a magazine that always interested him— the *International Dog Breeders Journal*. He thumbed through it looking for stories about chocolate Labrador retrievers. On page 38, where the advertisements began, he saw an ad which made him sit up straight in his scarlet and gray chair.

"Annabella, listen to this!" he exclaimed. "Some guy in Finland has a male chocolate Lab pup sired by Bubbling Bedouine for sale. He says it's the pick of the litter. The bitch is Tendercare Muskelunge Debbie; that dog is almost as famous as Bubbling Bedouine! We've got to have that pup!"

"What is he asking for it?" she said. "It's got to be expensive."

"It doesn't matter," he replied. "It's a male and anyway, whatever it is, we can afford it. Baby, we're going to Finland!"

Annabella had never been to Finland. If Ralph wanted to go to Finland to buy a dog, that was fine with her.

She thought a moment and then asked, "Ralphie, if we go to Finland, can I buy a reindeer pelt coat? I bet it would keep me really warm here in the winter." Annabella didn't know much about Finland, but she did know that reindeer lived there.

"Sure, you can get a reindeer coat, but we have to get the puppy first," Ralph said. "That's the reason we're going there."

"OK, well, what are we going to name it?" she asked. "It has to have a name, so we can get the travel documents for the puppy so we can bring him back."

"You're right, he has to have a name," said Ralph. "We'll name him after his father and his mother, so everyone will know who he came from. The name will be Tendercare Bubbling, uh, uh, something." Then a thought struck him. He jumped from his scarlet and gray chair, shouting, "I know, we'll name him Tendercare Bubbling Buckeye!"

And then Annabella said, "And we can call him 'Buckey' for short."

Within fifteen minutes, Ralph had Maddy Modulessi on the telephone. Maddy was in the whirlpool at his club, after a workout with a trainer which had been particularly strenuous. Maddy ran the largest liquor distribution business in Helsinki. He spent most evenings in bars throughout the city, promoting various liquors. He liked to exercise in the afternoon before starting his round of bar visits, which was why he was now in the whirlpool. It was unusual to take a phone call in the whirlpool, but Ralph had been so insistent with the young man at the front desk who had answered his call that the attendant brought the phone into the locker room. He found Maddy in the whirlpool, and gave him the phone.

The young man, whose name was Garvian, told Maddy, "Here, take this; this is some guy who really wants to talk to you and won't take no for an answer. He offered me a hundred dollars—what is that in Finnish marka, anyway? —to take the phone to you, so I thought it was important." Garvian still thought in terms of marka, even though Finland had adopted the euro in 2002.

Maddy was extremely annoyed with Garvian for expecting him to take a phone call while he was in the whirlpool. He almost threw the phone into the foaming water, but then thought the better of it. There was no sense in having to buy a new phone for the club.

He put the receiver to his ear, and said, "Who are you, and why are you calling me while I'm in a whirlpool?! And how in the heck did you find me here anyway?!"

Ralph had not realized the time difference, let alone having any idea he had called Maddy while he was in a whirlpool. While by now it was almost 8:00 a.m. in Shaker Heights, Ohio, it was almost 3:00 p.m. in Helsinki. And Ralph had not realized exactly what Maddy's wife had meant when she told him he was "exercising" when he had called Maddy's home telephone number, which was in the ad in the *International Dog Breeders Journal*. Ralph had only had his first cup of coffee that morning, and could be as daffy at times as his wife was ditzy. When Maddy told him he was "in a whirlpool," it didn't register with Ralph; he didn't know what that meant. He thought, oh my god, he's drowning in a whirlpool! He must be kayaking down a fjord, or something.

Ralph screamed into the phone, "I'm sorry, I'm sorry, hang up and call 911! Call 911!" Ralph then yelled to Annabella (which Maddy on the other end of the phone could also hear), "There are fjords in Finland, aren't there?!"

Maddy held the phone away from his ear. "Are you some kind of nut? Why should I call 911? Who are you, anyway?"

"I don't want you to drown in that whirlpool," replied Ralph. "I just want to buy your dog! If you drown, I'll never get him. Hang up and call 911!"

"I'm not drowning, you idiot! Now what do you want?"

Then Annabella yelled back at Ralph, "Fjords are in Norway, reindeer are in Finland!"

This was obviously not the best introduction Ralph could have made of himself to Maddy. However, to his credit, he did recover once he realized that Maddy was not drowning in a whirlpool. He explained who he was, and told Maddy he was interested in buying the puppy that Maddy had advertised in the *International Dog Breeders Journal*. Maddy too calmed down. He realized he probably had a sucker on the line who wanted to buy his dog, and mentally began increasing the price he was about to quote.

Once he understood what Ralph's call was all about, Maddy responded. "This is a great pup. He has the best chocolate color. I know dogs. I've been breeding chocolate Labs for 21 years, and I can tell which are the best pups. This one is not just the pick of the litter; he will be a *great* dog. He is beautiful, strong, and has an exuberant personality."

Ralph could hardly contain himself. "That's exactly what I want," he said. "How much does he cost? When can I get him?"

Well, that was probably not the best opening bargaining gambit. Ralph was way too enthusiastic.

Maddy adjusted the number in his head up a bit more, and said, "You know, Ralph, I don't know you other than by what you have told me on this call. But it sounds like you and Annabella have a nice home, and would be good dog owners for this extraordinary puppy. And you were genuinely concerned about me when you thought I was drowning in a whirlpool in a fjord, so I am going to give you a special deal, a deal I wouldn't normally give. I'll sell you the puppy for ten thousand euros."

Ralph didn't know how much that was. He had heard of euros, that was about it. He thought a euro was about the same as a dollar, and that seemed good enough for him. Ralph anticipated breeding Buckey (he was already calling him Buckey in his head) once he grew up, and expected to recoup most or all of whatever he had to pay for the dog fairly quickly. The money was not what was important; what was important was being able to brag to his friends that he owned a dog sired by Bubbling Bedouine. He quickly agreed to ten thousand euros. Maddy then said that they could pick up the puppy in three weeks, when he would be eight weeks old.

Three weeks later, Ralph and Annabella arrived at the Helsinki airport after a long flight from Cleveland, with a stop at London

Heathrow to change planes. They had left home at 2:20 p.m. the previous day, and it was now 6:15 a.m. in Helsinki. They had been travelling almost fifteen hours, much of it at night, and were tired and irritable. They went through customs and took a cab to their hotel, the Hilton Helsinki Kalastajatorppa. They had selected it because it was a "pet friendly" hotel and the travel brochure said it had a swimming pool and was close to the beach. Although he was afraid to mention the idea to his wife, Ralph halfway had visions of taking his new puppy to the beach to swim.

That afternoon, exhausted from their trip, they went to bed. Ralph was experiencing jet lag and both were suffering from the time zone change. They woke up at 4:00 a.m. They couldn't go back to sleep, so Ralph turned on the television. He flipped through the channels, but couldn't find any broadcasting in English.

"Ralphie," said Annabella, "turn that noise off. It all sounds like Chinese to me! I can't understand a thing they're saying!"

"Well, I'm pretty sure it's not Chinese," said Ralph. "We're in Finland, so they're probably speaking in Finn; it's definitely not Chinese. I'm going to call the hotel operator to check." Ralph picked up the telephone on the bedside table and dialed "0" for "operator."

After a long wait, a girl's voice answered, which Ralph thought sounded very much like the voices he and Annabella were hearing on the television.

"Pardon me," he said, when she finally paused in her greeting to him. "I know it is very early in the morning, unless this bedroom clock is wrong, but I wonder if you could tell me what language I am hearing on the television. It sounds like what you are saying too."

"Oh, sir," she said (in perfect English), "the language you are hearing on the television is *Suomi*, which is the language spoken by the majority of the population in Finland. If you want to hear the program in *English*, simply dial *3645474*—the numbers corresponding to English, on the keypad on your TV remote, and hit 'enter.' That will change the language you hear to English."

Ralph thanked her, and did as she instructed. Immediately, the television changed to English. Annabella was delighted, and tuned to the weather channel to see what the day would be like. The weathergirl announced with a smile that the day would be sunny with a high of 58 degrees.

Annabella was ecstatic. "This will be great day to meet Buckey," she exclaimed!

After eating breakfast in the café on the second floor mezzanine, they took the elevator to the ground floor of the hotel, where the doorman for the Hilton Helsinki Kalastajatorppa hailed a taxi for them. They instructed the driver to take them to Maddy's house on Kymintie Street on the northeast side of Helsinki, which turned out to be about a forty-five-minute ride, and cost sixty euros. Ralph grumbled about the fare, and then paid the taxi driver. He also made a deal for him to wait for them. They got out of the cab in front of the big rock which blocked their view of the house, and then followed the walk around it up to the front porch and front door.

Maddy had arranged for Alfonso and Mariana to be there with Tendercare Muskelunge Debbie and the puppy, so that Ralph and Annabella could meet the owners of Buckey's parents as well as his mother and the father when they got to meet their new puppy. Alfonso and Mariana brought their six kids as well. So it was quite a welcoming party that greeted them when they rang the bell and Maddy opened the door. It was hard to tell who was the most excited, Ralph and Annabella, or all the kids, who had never seen Americans before.

The three oldest came running, with Tymoco first shouting, "Welcome to Finland!" followed by Verviana, and Meganosa, with Feopatifus, Cynadita, and Lapaidacus, the youngest, and Maddy's kids, Marbelosa and Maffadaforus, bringing up the rear.

After an exchange of greetings and introductions, Maddy said, "Well, we all know you are anxious to see your new puppy. I'm going to ask my son, Maffadaforus, the youngest child here, to bring in the puppy. And Marbelosa, will you please bring in the proud father, Bubbling Bedouine, and you, Tymoco, please bring in the proud mother, Tendercare Muskelunge Debbie."

All three children turned and ran to the back of the house and out to the kennel to do as Maddy requested. They returned in a few minutes with the two dogs and the puppy.

Ralph and Annabella were enthralled. The dogs were beautiful! The puppy was the cutest puppy they had ever seen. Maffadaforus gently put him on the floor, and he immediately began running around, sniffing everyone in the room, and acting like he owned it. The two parents stood and watched him. Then the puppy ran over to Ralph and peed on Ralph's pant leg.

Maddy turned to Ralph and said, "He likes you, but he certainly has a mind of his own. It's obvious he thinks he is the top dog here, and he is only eight weeks old. You're going to have a fantastic dog; he is just like Bubbling was at that age. He is a one hundred percent alpha dog, and you'll really have to work with him if he is to learn that you are the top dog, and he isn't. Right now he thinks he is dominant over you—and everyone else, by the way. That isn't bad, it shows he has incredible confidence and spirit, but you'll need to work consistently to channel his spirit and energy in the right direction."

Ralph agreed, and said he couldn't be happier with the puppy. Annabella picked him up, and he peed on her too. She didn't care, at that moment she was enchanted with the cutest and most adorable puppy she had ever seen or held.

Ralph and Annabella admired the parents, Bubbling and Debbie. They had never seen such beautiful Labradors. The children all took turns holding the puppy. Ralph paid Maddy for the puppy with a ten-thousand-euro money order. Maddy asked what they would name him, and they told him the puppy's name was Tendercare Bubbling Buckeye. Maddy then went to his computer and entered the name on the appropriate papers. He hit the "send" button to send them to the Finnish National Kennel Club. Then he printed a copy of the pedigree, and gave it to Ralph. Next, they talked about Buckey's care and feeding. Finally, they all said goodbyes. Ralph and Annabella walked down the steps from the porch with Annabella carrying Buckey. The children crowded in the doorway to watch them leave. Tears were streaming down their faces as Ralph and Annabella disappeared from view behind the big rock. They heard the door of the taxi slam shut, and the engine roar as the cab started up and accelerated down the street. Somehow they knew they would never see Buckey again. The memory of watching his exuberance as he confidently explored his surroundings and his new world would not easily leave them.

Inside the taxi, Ralph opened the package of papers Maddy had given him. He looked at Buckey's pedigree, and a warm glow enveloped him. He knew he had paid a lot of money for Buckey, and now he knew the puppy was worth every penny he had cost. He looked at all the champions in his dog's background, and felt very, very good with himself.

This is the pedigree Maddy gave to Ralph:

Tendercare Bubbling Buckeye	Fin. CH Bubbling Bedouine	Fin. CH Exhibition Man De Saint Urbain	Mardas Maritime Man	Eng CH Mardas Master Mariner
				Timspring Eider
			Int., Fin., Eng., & Lux. CH Lejie Lucy	Eng CH Keysund Krispin of Blondella
				Lindall Miss Holly
		Fin. CH Loresho Oystercatcher	Fin. CH Charway Sea Badger	Eng Ch Kupros Master Mariner
				Charway Sally Brown
			Mallorn's Applesauce	Roseacre Madigan
				Fin. CH Sandy
	Tendercare Muskelunge Debbie	Am CH Banner's Muskelunge Buckeye	Banner's Wenwood Obleo	Am CH Beechcroft Edgewood Tomarc
				Wenwood's Banner Ruby Begonia
			Can CH Amblesides Banner of Triple L	Am CH Clemmsen of Killingworth
				Lindall Miss Emma
		Am CH Muskelunge's Devil's Advocate	Am CH Sir Duke of Muskelunge	Am CH Borador's Lord Travis
				Am CH Muskelunges Miss Sandalwood
			Sassafras's Black Devil	Am CH Muskelunge's Black Charmer
				Sal's Sassafras Of Muskelunge

CHAPTER 3

A NOSE FOR TROUBLE

Buckey missed his litter mates and his mother. Ralph and Annabella were OK; they made a big fuss over him, and they fed him more than he could eat of the food Maddy had given Ralph, but he felt lost and lonely. The hotel room at the Hilton Helsinki Kalastajatorppa was a strange place. Annabella had stopped playing with him, and was reading a book. Ralph was playing with the television, punching different language codes into the remote, to see how many languages it knew. The last one was *437626* for *German*, and Buckey didn't like the strange, guttural noise that now came from the television. He began to whimper and cry.

Annabella looked up from her book and asked, "Buckey, what's the matter?"

Ralph was engrossed with the television and seemingly oblivious to Buckey and Annabella.

"See," he said, "I've got it to translate *The Simpsons* into English, German, Italian, and Spanish. Remember, when you first turned it on? You thought you were hearing Chinese. I bet it even knows Chinese. Maybe some guy from Beijing was here before us and programmed the TV to talk in Chinese."

Annabella wasn't paying any attention to him.

She mumbled, "I'm going down the hall to get some ice and make a nice cold drink for Buckey." She got up and started to the door with the ice bucket.

Ralph was concentrating on the TV remote. He had punched in *2446 (for *Chin---) just as she opened the door. Neither of them was watching Buckey, who jumped up and followed Annabella into the hallway just before the door closed with a bang.

Annabella turned right to go down the hall to the ice machine, which was on the left side next to a vending machine in an alcove at the end of the hall. Buckey was immediately distracted by a smell coming from the other direction. He turned left and about ten doors further down stopped at a tray with two mostly eaten bowls of Nakkisoppa, which is a Finnish soup consisting of boiled, peeled potatoes, a few hot dogs, carrots, onions, and soup bouillon for flavor. It had been placed outside the door by two newlyweds, Glendaloca and Febber Rabberace, who were on their honeymoon. They had taken a break from their lovemaking to order two bowls of soup and a loaf of Nissua, a tender Finnish sweet bread made with cardamom, with sweet creamery butter from Denmark. After enjoying their bread and soup, they had put the tray with the dishes outside the door, placed a "Do not disturb" sign on the door handle, and resumed where they had left off. Buckey licked up all of the leftover soup. He thought it was delicious. Then he lifted his left leg, and began peeing in one of the bowls.

Twenty minutes earlier, a picky and somewhat obnoxious gentleman from Japan who had just arrived at the hotel, had gone to the room four doors further down the hall. He looked it over, and then angrily walked out with his luggage and went back down to the front desk. He proclaimed to the young lady behind the desk that he had reserved a room with a view of the bay, and that the room he was given lacked such a view. The young lady apologized profusely and gave him a different room. She then called housekeeping, and requested the chambermaid who answered the phone, Alita Allinghousen, to inspect the rejected room. Alita went to the room, saw everything was in order, and then left, entering the hallway just as Buckey was peeing into the soup bowl. Alita saw Buckey and screamed. She didn't really know what it was she saw, but she did see some animal peeing in the soup bowl. Lights in the hallway automatically dimmed at 9:00 p.m., and Buckey was of course chocolate in color and hard to make out against the dark green carpet in the dimly lit hallway. Alita started screaming because the first thought that came to her mind was that she saw a raccoon (even though Buckey didn't look anything like a raccoon). She knew that raccoons have very sharp teeth and claws, and can carry rabies, and are very dangerous. A wave of fear came over her, and her piercing screams could be heard the length of the hall.

Glendaloca and Febber had an immediate case of interruption of activities [lat.: co.int.].

As they jumped from the bed Glendaloca exclaimed "What's that?!"

"Someone is being attacked," yelled Febber. "You get under the bed! I'm going to see what's going on!" Febber raced to the door and flung it open, totally forgetting that he was not wearing any clothes.

Alita began screaming even louder—yelling at him to go away. She wasn't afraid of a nude man, but she was trying to alert him and save him from being clawed by the raccoon. "Get away, get away!" she screamed. Her screams were now heard by guests on the floor above as well as the floor below.

Saeya Wimmellton was in the room directly above and also heard Alita's screams. She ran to the phone, dialed 9 for an outside line, and called 112 (which is the number you call in Finland in an emergency, like 911 in the United States). Speaking loudly and rapidly in a panicky, excited voice she told the operator either some woman was being attacked, or there must be a fire in the hotel. The operator quickly dispatched the Helsinki City Rescue Department. Within four minutes three fire engines and one hook and ladder truck arrived at the front of the hotel, sirens blaring and completely blocking the street.

Annabella had finished getting ice out of the ice machine. It had been a laborious process, since someone had already taken most of it. She didn't know it, but the ice had been taken by Nanamamus Maxipekopolis, a very successful young man from Greece, who had invited some friends, male and female, to a party at the hotel. He had taken most of the ice in a cooler, to ice down a case of Grolsch beer.

More on him later. Annabella was only able to get a few cubes at a time out of the machine, and gave up trying for more when her ice bucket was only half full. She had just come out of the alcove housing the ice and vending machines and started down the hallway when Alita began screaming. And at that moment she also saw Buckey running toward her down the hallway.

The screaming really scared Buckey. He had never heard anything like it, and had immediately started running in the other direction. He saw Annabella, a familiar figure. Annabella tossed the ice bucket to one side, scooped Buckey up in her arms, and quickly got back to their own room. Ralph was angry that Buckey was missing, totally relieved that he was back, and full of questions. He too heard Alita's screaming, but was too concerned about Buckey and Annabella to pay any attention to it.

A few minutes later, they could hear people running in the hallway. These were the firemen from the Helsinki City Rescue Department. Then they heard a loud thud! One of the firemen had slipped on the ice from Annbella's ice bucket; his feet went up in the air, and his butt hit the floor hard. A minute or so later, there was a loud knock! knock! knock! on the door. Ralph opened the door, and it was one of the firemen.

"We're checking all the rooms in this area" he said. "Is there any fire in here?"

"Absolutely not," replied Ralph.

"Also," the fireman asked, "Have any of you seen a raccoon in your room?"

"A raccoon! Are you crazy?" said Ralph. "There's nothing in this room except me, my wife and Buckey here, and he's not a raccoon!"

Just a few moments before Buckey peed in the soup bowl, a little over three kilometers away on the other side of Helsinki, Robbier Rafferty was pulling himself up a rope to the roof above the top floor of the offices of Handelsbanken. This was the home office of a Finnish bank which had 774 other offices in 24 countries around the globe. The home office was located at Aleksanterinkatu 11, in an upscale commercial area of the city just down the street from the Helsinki Cathedral and Senate Square.

Robbier was a professional thief. He had learned a lot about the bank from a young lady he had dated who had worked at the bank, but who had been dismissed from her job. For several months he had carefully developed his plan to rob the Handelsbanken. Entering the bank was the easy part. He had spent an hour or so one night a week earlier unsealing the roof window, and then carefully replacing it, but leaving it so it could be opened easily and quickly. His plan called for him to come back at a later time, enter the bank through the roof window, steal as much cash as he could find and carry, and also steal the codes to the safes in each of the other offices of the bank, and leave. Later he would rob other offices of the bank at his convenience.

That night he was up on the roof, checking around for anything unusual, when the sirens from the Helsinki City Rescue Department fire vehicles went off. All these sirens went off at an opportune time for Robbier. He thought to himself, he couldn't have a better distraction. He opened the roof window and lowered himself and two suitcases down into the room below.

Once inside the bank, Robbier knew exactly what he wanted to do and how to do it. He quickly went to the president's office. He took down the picture of the founder of the bank which was on the wall behind the president's big desk, and went to work opening the wall safe hidden behind the picture. He pressed a key on his smart phone which was programmed to emit a series of tones, one of which could unlock the digital safe. Within a minute and a half, one of the random code tones hit, and the display on the safe flashed green. Robbier opened the door to the safe. Just as he had figured, the codes for all of the other bank safes were in the wall safe, as well as the code for the cash vault in the home office bank. Robbier made copies of the codes using the copier next to the desk used by the president's secretary, outside his big office. Using his smart phone, he also then made copies of the digital tone codes which were on a separate transmitting device that controlled the safes in all of the bank's offices. He carefully replaced what he had taken from the wall safe, closed it, and put the picture back on the wall. When he left, the office looked like nothing had happened.

Robbier went to the basement floor, found the cash vault, and went to work to open it using the codes he had stolen. Opening the safe required opening both a mechanical lock, which he was able to do with the numerical cash vault code he had copied, and a digital lock, which opened with one of the tones he had recorded on his smart phone. It took him less than three minutes to open the vault. Then he filled both of his suitcases with stacks of one-hundred euro notes, closed the vault, and returned to the top floor of the building.

He tied the end of his rope to the suitcases, climbed the rope to the roof, and then pulled up the suitcases. Then he replaced the window. He used the rope to lower the suitcases to the ground in an alley behind the bank. Then, after doubling it around a water pipe with both ends hanging to the ground, he rappelled down the side of the building to the ground. Tugging on one end, he pulled the rope to the ground and carried the rope and the two suitcases to an old Saab he had stolen earlier in the evening. The owner had carelessly left the keys in the car, making it easy to steal. Robbier had left the car parked in the shadows in the alley. Robbier put the suitcases and the rope in the trunk, got in the driver's seat, threw his hat into the back seat, and drove to the Helsinki airport. No one had seen him, no alarms had sounded, and his plan had come off perfectly.

Or so he thought. What he did not know was that the cash vault in the bank had been programmed to automatically send a text message to the president of the bank each time it opened.

When Robbier arrived at the airport, he parked the car on the top floor of the parking garage opposite terminal two. He felt exhilarated with how successful his plan had gone to that point. He jumped out of the car and took the suitcases out of the trunk. He locked the car, picked up the suitcases, and carried them over the walkway to terminal two. He went to the service floor, where the Hotel GLO Helsinki Airport is located, and walked straight to the reception desk. At that point it was 10:45 p.m.

"I'd like a room for tonight, please, if you have any rooms left," he said to the young clerk on duty.

"You're definitely in luck," she said. This hotel has seventy-six rooms, sir, and we are practically sold out, but we do still have one room available. There's only one thing I must tell you about it; it's a handicap room, which means it has handrails all around the bathroom walls, the toilet is a high toilet, and both the door to the room and the bathroom door are wider than normal, to accommodate a wheelchair. Some people don't like that, but it's the only room we have available tonight. And it's next to the sauna. Would you like to book it?"

Robbier said the handicap room was OK with him and that since he had an early flight, he would pay for it right then. Robbier didn't really plan to get on an early flight; he just didn't want to go back to the reception desk to check out when he left the next morning. He took his two suitcases to the room. He used the bathroom (the toilet *was* high; his feet didn't reach the floor when he sat on the commode), took a shower, and went to bed.

The next morning, he left the room with his suitcases at about eight o'clock and went to the ticket counter which was on the second floor of the terminal. He looked at the screen showing departing flights, and quickly scanned all the flights. He was looking for one going to the United States, preferably not to a gateway city like New York. He spotted a US Airways flight that was leaving for Cleveland Ohio, USA, at 10:15 a.m. Robbier went to the counter and asked to buy a ticket to Cleveland, Ohio. He was able to get on the US Airways flight. He paid cash for his ticket with twelve of the one hundred euro bills he had earlier taken out of one of his suitcases. The agent asked if he had any baggage to check, and he said, yes, he wanted to check two bags. He had to pay twenty-five euros extra to check the bags, because one was two kilos over the weight limit of 23 kilos. The agent put baggage tags on his two suitcases and told him to take them to the security line for screening.

Just as Robbier was turning away and bending over to pick up his suitcases, an officer with the Finnish National Bureau of Investigation rushed up to the airline counter and called for the ticket agents to gather around.

"There has been a major bank robbery!" he said. "We are monitoring all outgoing flights, particularly flights to London, Amsterdam, Paris and New York."

He continued on with instructions to the agents, but Robbier didn't wait around to hear them. He headed toward the screening area with his two suitcases. He thought, Oh, oh, how did this happen? This is big trouble; I've got to get rid of these suitcases, quick. As he approached the bag screening area he noticed that both of the security agents who took bags and put them on the belt to go through the screener had left the front of the screener and had moved about twenty feet toward the counter so they could hear the FNBI officer. That officer was continuing to give detailed instructions to the ticket agents as to what to look for in light of the bank robbery. The two security agents who were working the conveyor belt now had their backs to the belt and the screening machine.

Robbier saw an opportunity and quickly moved into the area just vacated by the two security agents. There were several bags in front of the screening machine, waiting to be placed on the conveyor. Robbier saw two bags with tags showing they were going to CLE (the airport code for Cleveland). He bent over as though depositing his own bags and in a flash with his pocket knife deftly slit the tag on one of the bags underneath the bag handle, and yanked it off. He did the same thing with the tag on one of his bags, and then switched them, placing the tag from someone else's bag on his own.

He was about to remove the tag on the next bag, when he heard the officer, who was speaking quite loudly, saying, "That's all now, we're counting on all of you to help us find this bank robber. Go back to work and watch for anything suspicious!"

Robbier immediately stopped what he was doing and slipped into the crowd of travelers that was moving through the terminal past the bag screening area.

Ralph, and Annabella who was carrying Buckey, had dropped their two bags at the bag screening area only a few moments earlier. Then they proceeded toward the security control area. They didn't hear the officer who was telling the ticket agents about a bank robbery, and they didn't see Robbier take the tag from one of their bags. They got to the security area and waited in the long line. When it was their turn, they showed their passports and tickets to the officer. They were on US Airlines flight 782 to Cleveland, Ohio, USA, travelling first class. They had purchased a seat for Buckey, who because he was under eighteen pounds, was permitted to ride in the passenger cabin. They produced his ticket as well, and the papers Maddy had given them showing that he was their dog. The agent waved them through to the line to the X-ray machine.

Buckey had to go through the machine by himself, and he went first. The usually stern officer directing passengers into the machine broke into a big smile when he saw Buckey. He bent over to pet him, and at that moment Buckey darted between the man's legs and ran through the machine. The officer whirled around as he was straightening up and banged his head on the edge of the X-Ray machine. He hit so hard it knocked him silly, and he fell to his knees. Buckey ran into the concourse beyond the security area and disappeared in the crowd of passengers. Ralph and Annabella, on the other side of the X-Ray machine, were frantic. They started screaming at the security agent, who at this point was lying on the floor in the middle of the X-Ray machine.

This of course attracted a lot of attention. The agents on the opposite side of the conveyor belt came running over, guns drawn. One of them yelled at Annabella, "Shut up, and put your hands above your head!"

Two others were trying to pick up the officer who had banged his head. He was overweight and very heavy, and they struggled to lift him. The passengers in the line were all craning their necks, trying to see what had happened. One passenger further back in the line was Robbier Rafferty. He was next in line to have his documents checked. When all the confusion started, the agent at the small desk there also ran to the conveyor belt area. Not thinking, she dropped her stamp on the desk when she turned to go to the X-Ray machine area. Robbier picked it up, stamped his own ticket, and cut in further up the line. The other passengers were all concentrating on the commotion at the front of the line, and nobody paid any attention to him.

Back at the bag screening area, one of the security officers had started to put Robbier Rafferty's bag with the switched tag onto the belt leading to the X-Ray machine. This was the heavier bag, the one for which Robbier had to pay twenty-five euros extra because it was over the weight limit.

He thought, this is an awfully heavy bag; maybe I should check it by hand. Most bags just went through the machine; only a few, on a random basis, were opened and checked by hand. The officer put the bag on a table, opened it, and was aghast when he saw it was packed with bundles of one hundred euro notes. He sucked in his breath, and then yelled for the FNBI agent. The one that had given instructions to the ticket agents came running and when he saw the money, summoned three other FNBI agents on his radio. He then removed the tag on the bag and took it to the ticket counter.

"Quickly, look up the name of the passenger who has this bag!" he barked at the ticket agent.

In a moment, the somewhat terrified middle aged lady agent behind the counter told him, "That bag ticket is for Ralph Rapaski, on US Airlines flight 782 to Cleveland Ohio."

The four FNBI agents ran toward the security screening area, where the commotion was about over. Meanwhile, the agent who had hit his head was telling the others he had not been attacked by Annabella or anyone else; he just hit his head when he was getting up after trying to pet a dog.

As everyone was going back to their posts, the FNBI agents arrived at the scene, and one of them asked in a very loud voice, "Is there a Ralph Rapaski in this line?!"

Ralph raised his hand, and immediately was swarmed over by the four agents. They took him and Annabella to a small room adjacent to the security area and ordered them to stand facing the wall with their hands against it. Then they searched them. Ralph was both terrified and angry.

"What is going on?" he demanded. "We didn't do anything. We don't have any drugs. And that agent back there lost our dog! That is a very expensive dog! We gotta get out of here and try to find him!"

It took about fifteen minutes for the agents to come to the conclusion that they had nothing to do with the bank robbery. While they were being interrogated, another agent arrived and informed the others that a security camera behind the bank had captured a picture of a man getting into an old Saab in the alley behind the bank, not long after the time the cash vault at the bank had opened. Ralph didn't look like the man in the picture; he was too short and overweight. Also, the license plate on the old Saab was visible in the image captured by the security camera, and the car with that plate had been found on the top floor of the parking garage at the airport. Ralph had the receipt from his rental car, which showed how he had come to the airport. The FNBI agent had opened and searched the Saab, and found a hat in the back seat, which he produced. The hat was too small for Ralph's head. The FNBI agents apologized to Ralph and Annabella for detaining them.

Ralph, Annabella and the four FNBI agents left the small interrogation room to find Buckey. They fanned out and started down the concourse corridor, looking in every shop, newsstand, eating area, coffee shop, and gate waiting area along the way. They almost missed Buckey. Halfway down the corridor was a shoe shine stand, with two chairs. Buckey was sitting on one of the chairs. He had gotten tired of wandering around the concourse, and had come up to the shoe shine girl, who thought he looked adorable. She had picked him up and petted him, and then placed him in one of the two vacant chairs when a customer came up to get a shoe shine. The customer got into the other chair. Buckey liked the shoe shine girl and was very content to sit in the chair and watch her swish her brush and shoe rag over the man's shoes. The man getting his shoes shined picked up a newspaper and began reading it, ignoring Buckey.

Annabella had just walked past the shoeshine stand without noticing Buckey, who was partially hidden from view by the newspaper. He caught her scent, however, and when he looked up from the shoe shine girl and saw Annabella, he gave a short "woof!" Annabella turned and saw Buckey, and rushed to him with a huge sense of relief. She called for Ralph, who came running with the four FNBI agents. Ralph also was overwhelmed with relief at having found Buckey.

"Gosh," he said, "I'm glad that's over, and we found him. We sure have had enough excitement for one day."

"We're going to miss our plane!" said Annabella. "What gate do we go to?"

"Your flight is at gate B-12," said one of the agents. "We'll take you there, and I'll call ahead and tell them to hold the flight for you."

Then one of the other agents said, "You know, that is a great looking dog. He's a Lab, isn't he?"

Ralph said yes, and added that Buckey was a purebred Lab with an illustrious father, Bubbling Bedouine.

"I understand Labs have a great sense of smell," said the agent. "Maybe Buckey can help us catch the bank robber."

Ralph said he was agreeable to let Buckey try, and they all proceeded to Gate B-12.

All the other passengers had already boarded the plane. One of the flight attendants was waiting at the door for them, and ushered them into the first class cabin. Ralph and Annabella had seats 4A and 4B, and Buckey had seat 4C, which was an aisle seat in the middle section. The four FNBI agents came on the plane with them, and one of them quickly explained to the flight attendant that they believed there was a bank robber on board, and they would have to search the plane. While he was explaining the situation to the flight attendant, another agent was showing Buckey the hat that had been taken from the back seat of the Saab in the parking garage. Buckey sniffed the hat, and the agent put it away.

Then Ralph told Buckey, "find it!"

Buckey jumped out of seat 4C, and started running up and down the aisle in the first class section, going back and forth from one side to the next. Then he went down the other first class aisle doing the same thing. One of the passengers, an elderly man in seat 6F, on the other side of the plane, rang his call button and reported to a flight attendant that a dog was loose on the airplane. The flight attendant gently informed him that it was OK, not to worry about it, and that the dog was only trying to find a bank robber.

The elderly man replied, "Oh, really? I guess it's OK then."

Not all of the passengers were quite so accommodating as Buckey made his way back through the plane. There had been no announcement of what was going on, so as not to eliminate the element of surprise should Buckey in fact find the bank robber. The FNBI agents didn't want whoever it was to know they were about to capture him (assuming he was on the plane!). As Buckey went through the coach section of the plane, he went under the legs of the passengers in the aisle and middle seats, so he could sniff the passenger sitting next to the window. As he went under the back of the legs of a lady sitting in seat 14C the fur on the top of his back tickled her legs and she jumped. She turned to the man next to her and slapped his face with the back of her hand.

"Keep your hands to yourself!" she angrily told him, thinking he had attempted to feel her up.

The man drew back in horror. He said, "Lady, I didn't touch you!" Then he looked down and saw Buckey. "There, look at that!"

"Get out of here!" she yelled in the direction of Buckey.

The passenger on the other side of the aisle, who heard all of this, thought there must be some domestic argument going on between a husband and wife. "Why don't you two do your arguing in your own house!" he said.

"I'm not married to *him*!" replied the lady who had been touched by Buckey.

And the man next to her said, "And I'm not married to *her* either, and I wouldn't marry her for all the gold in China!"

At that, she slapped him again!

Buckey had finished with row 14 and now was at row 15, sniffing each passenger. As he moved along, he frequently would brush a passenger's legs, causing them to jump. It was almost like people would "elevate" an inch or so as Buckey passed under their legs. The ladies with bare legs, like the lady in seat 14C, got a particular thrill from this, and all had different reactions. Most were just a small "Ooough!"

Or a "What is that!" Or, "Aagh, something tickled me!" No one else, however, reacted as badly as the lady in Seat 14C.

Robbier Rafferty was in seat 27A, further back in the plane. He had heard the commotion up ahead in row 14, and watched as passengers in the subsequent rows seemed to jump up a bit, one after another. He sensed something was not right, and his pulse began to race. He nervously observed the unusual activity get closer and closer to his row. When Buckey got to row 27, he smelled Robbier in seat 27A, a window seat. Robbier had the same scent that Buckey had smelled on the hat shown to him by the FNBI agent. Buckey began to bark, and at that moment, the FNBI agents started rushing down the aisle.

Robbier knew he had to get out of the plane, quick, but how? He pulled a bundle of one hundred euro notes that he had taken with him out of his coat pocket, removed the band, and flung them forward and toward the aisle. In an instant, money appeared to be raining from the ceiling. Passengers jumped up and into the aisle to grab the one hundred euro notes. People were screaming and pushing each other, each trying to get as many of the notes as possible. The FNBI agents were trapped in the melee. Immediately after creating the distraction, Robbier began crawling over the "A" seat backs toward the front, and when he was past the mass of passengers fighting over the euro notes, eased into the aisle and began running to the front.

An FNBI agent who had been pushed backward and spun around spotted him and yelled (although at that moment he couldn't even get close to Robbier), "Stop, you're under arrest!"

Further up in the plane, the only passengers who knew what was going on were Ralph and Annabella, because Ralph had been accused of being the bank robber. When Ralph heard the FNBI agent yell, he rushed down the aisle to stop Robbier. Ralph had played football in high school, and even though he was a bit overweight, was still pretty quick. He ran down the first class aisle, tackled Robbier just as he was about to reach the exit door, and fell on top of him. Then the FNBI agents who had broken free from the melee over the euro notes arrived. One had picked up Buckey, and the other three grabbed Robbier.

"You're under arrest!" one said, and the other two put Robbier's arms behind him and handcuffed him. Then they led him off the airplane.

There was a further delay while the airline baggage crew searched the baggage area of the plane for Robbier's bag. After they found and removed it, the plane was cleared to leave. Ralph, Annabella, and Buckey settled in for the long flight to Cleveland. Buckey went to sleep in his chair, seat 4C. He was tired. He had had a big day. Buckey and Ralph were both given commendations by the FNBI. Buckey didn't know it, but he was now a famous dog. He had caught the notorious professional bank robber, Robbier Rafferty, and that would profoundly alter the direction of his life.

Buckey's new life began the next day, when they arrived at Ralph and Annbella's house in Shaker Heights. Buckey liked his new home with them. He got to play with lots of other Labrador retrievers and he learned all the basic things a dog needs to learn from humans, because Ralph and Annabella spent a lot of time with him. He grew up fast, and by 11 months old had attained his full growth and weighed almost 80 pounds. He also had a lot to do. He had received a lot of publicity after the flight from Helsinki, and law enforcement agencies from many jurisdictions started asking for his help, in emergencies, or to track a fugitive or a thief. These included not just the police department in Shaker Heights, but also the Cleveland Police Department and many others, and even the Federal Bureau of Investigation. Buckey was the best dog any of them had ever used for tracking people. Lots of dogs can find things, like drugs in suitcases at the airport, or in a car stopped by police. But not many can be given a scent, and then track wherever it went, or find it again in a remote place. Buckey excelled at these tasks, and helped find lost children, lost valuables, and criminals and fugitives, just as he had done on the flight from Helsinki. Each time he did this, he got more publicity, which resulted in more requests for his services.

At the same time, Ralph of course wanted Buckey to sire offspring, and after he was a year old he was regularly given that duty as well. He was a very busy young dog. This entire book could be about Buckey, because he solved many exciting and interesting cases with his nose. But it isn't, so now is time to move on to another part of the story.

CHAPTER 4

GRANDFATHER SKAGGS

The M/S Viking Libertarian was on a voyage from Kotka, Finland to Cleveland, Ohio. The voyage had taken it through the Gulf of Finland, past Helsinki, into the Baltic Sea south of Copenhagen, then north through the Great Belt on the east side of Denmark, and into the North Sea. From there it had sailed northwest to the Port of Inverness in Scotland, to unload eight cords of the finest Finnish packaged birch timber to be made into toothpicks and thread spools by the Scottish firm Pick-A-Tee, Ltd. It then proceeded around the north of Scotland, south of the Faroe Islands and Iceland. It continued through the North Atlantic past Greenland and now was headed to Labrador, where the captain had decided to stop at Red Bay. After that stop, it would continue through the Strait of Belle Isle and head into the Gulf of St. Lawrence, passing the two great cities of Quebec City and Montreal on its way up the St. Lawrence River to Lake Ontario. It would then traverse a series of locks and canals, on the west side of Niagara Falls, to get to Lake Erie. After crossing that shallowest of the Great Lakes it would arrive at the third largest port in the Great Lakes, the Port of Cleveland, at the mouth of the Cuyahoga River.

The fact that the M/S Viking Libertarian was on this journey can be traced to a party that was held in the Hilton Helsinki Kalastajatorppa several months earlier. Nanamamus Maxipekopolis, a young Greek who had inherited a substantial sum of money and who was trying to establish a shipping business, had been staying in the hotel. He was trying to negotiate deals to transport forest products on the two medium size cargo ships he had purchased with most of his inheritance. His plan was to establish a regular route between Athens, Greece, and Helsinki, transporting Greek cement north to Helsinki, and Finnish goods back to Athens. He thought that the Athens-Helsinki route was underserved and that it would be a good opportunity for getting his business started. Although he was focusing on forest products, he had heard that a tractor company was looking for a cargo ship, and so he paid a visit to the company.

When Nanamamus arrived at the Valta Tractor Company, he met Safiina Kaapriella, the receptionist. Safiina was a knockout, drop dead gorgeous, twenty-two-year-old blonde. She told him she would get him an appointment with the marketing VP, who made decisions about shipping and distribution, but it would have to be the next day. Although he had come for an appointment with a VP, after Nanamamus saw Safiina his mind was only on her. He thought to himself, I bet this chick has heard every come-on line in the book; what the heck can I say to try to get her to go out with me?

He said, "Thank you, thank you. I can come back tomorrow." He then baited his hook, "That will be very helpful to me."

"OK, I have you down for 11:30 a.m.," said Safiina. "See you then."

Nanamamus dangled the hook in front of her, "You know, I'm new to Helsinki; I'm from Athens, Greece, and I'm just learning my way around here. I've met a number of people, like you, who gave me contacts and introductions to help get my cargo business started."

"Yeah?" she said.

"So I thought, what can I do in return?" he continued. "I'm hosting a small party at the Hilton Helsinki Kalastajatorppa hotel this Friday, after work, for some of these people. I want to invite you, if you can come. It's for a group of interesting business people, like yourself."

Safiina was a little taken aback. She was uncertain as to how to respond. The hook was in her mouth, or at least in front of it, but she hadn't swallowed it.

"What time is your party?" she asked, not backing away from the hook.

"We'll gather at eight o'clock, and it will be in room 3005 in the hotel," said Nanamamus. "You can stay for as long or as little as you like, but it would really be nice if you came."

He then set the hook, "You've been very helpful to me as a struggling young businessman just starting out. You can't believe how hard it is to get your feet off the ground in this business. You may not think it's much, but the help I've gotten from you and the others who will be there is so important, you just don't know how much it means to me."

At that, Safiina had just about swallowed the hook. She was caught, at least for going to this party. At this point she couldn't refuse. "OK, I'll come to your party," she said.

Nanamamus thanked her and turned to go, but before he got to the door, she had a second thought, and said, "Oh, by the way, can I bring a friend?"

Nanamamus was startled. Then he replied, "Sure, no problem."

It was the only thing he could say, and anyway, maybe she would bring a friend as good looking as herself. He left congratulating himself on getting this knockout bombshell to come to his hotel on Friday. Now he had to do something to create a "party."

Nanamamus had met a number of people during his stay in Helsinki, but really didn't know anyone he could invite to a party. So on Friday at seven-thirty p.m., he went to the Vista Bar and Lounge on the first floor of the hotel and talked to two couples sitting at the bar. By sheer coincidence, one of the couples happened to be Cecilia and Wisfusen, two of the handlers at the Helsinki Dog Show. They were now dating, and out for an evening of fun with two friends. Nanamamus told them there was a party in half an hour in Room 3005, with free drinks and hors d'oeuvres, and that they should come up and join in.

"Great, we'll be there!" said Cecilia.

Nanamamus went back to his room, iced down a case of Grolsch (this was just before Annabella tried to get ice out of the same ice machine, to make a cold drink for Buckey!), and opened a bottle of

Ouzo. He also put out on the desk an open can of sardines and a box of saltine crackers.

Promptly at eight o'clock, the two couples from the bar arrived. They all knew each other and continued their conversation where they had left off, only now they were drinking Nanamamus' beer and wine. Five minutes later, there was a knock on the door. Nanamamus opened it, and Safiina walked in, followed by a young man.

"Hi. You said I could bring a friend. This is Gustave Neiderbaum, my boyfriend," she said.

Nanamamus felt the energy drain from his body. He was expecting her to bring a good-looking girlfriend, but Safiina had just introduced him to a big strong handsome guy!

Recovering quickly, he said, "Hey, nice to meet you, come on in." He tried his best not to show his disappointment, and decided to strike up a conversation with Gustave, to see where it would go.

"Gustave, what do you do?" he asked.

"I just got my Sea Captain license last month," he replied. "I studied at the Helsinki Maritime School so I could take the tests. Now I'm looking for work or maybe an apprenticeship so I can upgrade my license to larger ships."

"Oh, yeah? That's interesting," said Nanamamus. "We have something in common. You know, I'm Greek, and my family's been in shipping for generations. I've got two ships now and I'm trying to get started in the cargo business."

He paused, and then said, "How did you get into this? And why did you want to be a Sea Captain?"

"I'm from Oulu," Gustave replied, "on the north coast of the Baltic Sea, about six hundred kilometers from here. It is about seven hours by road. The most famous person ever to come from Oulu was Gustave Ferdinand Niebaum, a Finnish Sea Captain. He was a great fur trader and explorer, and founded the Alaskan Commercial Company in San Francisco. He was sort of my idol."

"Really?" said Nanamamus. "What else did he do?"

"Well, he mapped some of the Alaskan coastline for the first time ever. In 1867, he was the Consul of Russia in the United States, when

Finland was part of Russia. He was involved in the purchase of Alaska by the United States from Russia. And he established the Inglenook Winery in California. His wine won gold medals at the World's Fair of Paris in 1889. Francis Ford Coppola purchased the winery in 1975 with proceeds from the Godfather movie."

"That's amazing," said Nanamamus, "that a guy from such a small far-away place could do all that. Amazing! And you want to do something like he did?"

"Well, I just want to be a sea captain," said Gustave. "My mother, Genevieve, grew up in Oulu near the sea, and she heard about Gustave Niebaum all her life. When I was born she wanted me to also grow up to be a famous sea captain, and that's why I was named Gustave and not Niilo after my dad, which is what he wanted. He has never let me forget that he thought I should have been named Niilo. I'm glad I wasn't; I like Gustave a lot better. And now I'm a Sea Captain, like Gustave Niebaum."

He thought for a moment, and then said, "So you're in shipping? How's that going?"

"My grandfather was Aristotle Maxipekopolis," said Nanamamus. "Shipping is in our family's blood. I was able to buy a couple of cargo ships, and I'm here to drum up some business. I want to establish regular routes so the ships can go back and forth between the same ports with cargo each way. One of the problems to avoid is empty return trips. I can transport Greek cement to Finland, and I want to fill the ships for the return trips."

At that point Safiina jumped in, and said, "Wait a minute. I've heard about Greek belly dancing, and all the tourists going there to the Greek islands, but I've never heard of Greek cement. What are you talking about, anyway?"

Nanamamus picked up the challenge, "What are the most famous things you think of when someone mentions Athens, Greece?"

"Well," said Safiina, "I suppose the Parthenon, and all the Greek ruins that people go to see."

"Right," said Nanamamus, "and all those ruins are made of limestone. And limestone is what cement is made from. Greece is nothing but one big limestone rock. And it is the cement capital of the world, well, it could be anyway. There is more cement made there than anywhere else. And I'm going to ship it all over the world."

Safiina didn't have a response to that, but she was starting to think, this sounds like a lot of bullshit!

All of a sudden Nanamamus had what he thought was a brilliant idea.

He said to Gustave, "Say, maybe we can do business together. I'm about to buy another ship, and I need to find a sea captain. If you are interested in the job, give me your phone number and I'll call you in a couple of days."

Gustave said that would be great, and gave him his number.

The idea that had suddenly come into Nanamamus' head was a plan to get Gustave out of the way, so he could move in on Safiina who was just standing there taking this all in. Three days earlier, Nanamamus had seen the following article in one of the daily newspapers, the *Helsinki Sanomat*:

HELSINKI, Finland (AP) — The Finnish authorities on Wednesday impounded 160 tons of explosives and 69 surface-to-air Patriot missiles that were found on a Panamanian flagged cargo ship. While the ship's ultimate destination was stated to be Shanghai, officials said, it was not clear where the weapons were bound.

The cargo ship, M/S Viking Liberty, sailed from the Dutch port of Rotterdam on Dec. 16, and two days later docked in Kotka, Finland, to pick up a cargo of anchor chains, said a Finnish Customs spokesman, Petri Loudenatmaa.

Investigating officers did not know the origin of the missiles or who was supposed to receive them, Mr. Loudenatmaa said.

"We have impounded the explosives and missiles and asked the Defense Ministry to transport and store them," he said. At this point, he said, it had not been determined if the Viking Liberty planned a drop before its port of destination in China.

The government has instituted proceedings to seize the ship as well, as its documents appear to be fraudulent and its origin and ownership cannot be determined.

Nanamamus had thought to himself, I'm going to buy that ship at auction, and put Gustave on it as sea captain, and then send him as far away from here as I can send him!

Cecilia interrupted the conversation. She said to Gustave, "We couldn't help overhearing that you're a sea captain from Oulu. That's a great fishing area for herring and sprat. Are you going to be a captain of a fishing boat?"

Gustave said that he was interested in that, and if he could ever get enough money together to buy a boat he would want to do that.

"Well, if you do," said Cecilia, "you should get yourself a good Labrador retriever dog. The fishermen in Labrador train them to help pull in the nets. They love to pull. They are very strong, can stand the cold, and are excellent swimmers."

Gustave thought that was a good idea, and filed it away for the time he might be able to have his own fishing boat.

About then everyone heard a bunch of sirens. No one knew what was going on, but it was like a dash of cold water. Cecilia and Wisfusen felt unnerved, and made an excuse to leave. The party quickly broke up. Safiina thought to herself as she left with Gustave, maybe that guy Nanamamus is not such a jerk after all. That had been a thought nagging at her ever since she had agreed to go to his party. She really couldn't decide. Nevertheless, she was glad she had asked Gustave, an old childhood friend, to go with her and pose as her boyfriend.

On Monday, the Polish crew of the seized ship M/S Viking Liberty, who had been apprehended, were released on bail. How they came up with the bail money was unknown. They then disappeared. No one appeared to claim ownership of the vessel, and in a matter of days the Finnish government obtained a court order seizing the ship and scheduled an auction to sell it. Pledging his two cargo ships as collateral, Nanamamus arranged a large loan from the Handelsbanken, which he used to submit the high and winning bid at the auction. In the opinion of experienced ship brokers who attended he vastly overpaid for the Viking Liberty, which was not in very good condition and lacked modern navigation electronics.

Nanamamus renamed the vessel Viking Libertarian (that made it easy to change the name, with a minimum of paint). The next day he called Gustave, and arranged a meeting. He offered him a job as sea captain on the vessel, to take a load of cargo to Cleveland, Ohio. He had underbid another shipping company to take a load of drilling equipment to Cleveland, which was the furthest cargo destination he could find. The drilling equipment was for fracking natural gas, and was being sent for use in opening a new offshore natural gas field that had been discovered in shale deposits underlying Lake Erie. It was all ready to be loaded on the ship, and the shipper was in a big hurry to have it delivered. Gustave agreed to be sea captain for the voyage, asking for half of his fee in advance, with the other half to be paid when he returned. Nanamamus was delighted; there would be no delay in getting Captain Gustave out of the way, and he would be gone for a long time, as it was a very long trip to Cleveland, Ohio and back.

The eight cords of birch lumber were a last minute addition to the M/S Viking Libertarian's cargo, as a favor to a timber mill whose business Nanamamus was courting. After he had dropped the birch at the Port of Inverness in Scotland for the Pick-A-Tee company, and headed across the North Atlantic, Captain Gustave had time to think. He began to contemplate what he would try to do after this voyage. He thought working for Nanamamus would not lead anywhere; he expected him to go bankrupt. He had heard how much Nanamamus overpaid for the Viking Libertarian, and he had the bill of lading for the drilling equipment which he was carrying. He could easily see that Nanamamus was going to lose his shirt on the deal. He was glad he got half of his pay in advance, and thought he would be lucky if he got the other half when he returned.

As he proceeded across the North Atlantic, Gustave contemplated buying a trawler for fishing the Baltic Sea upon his return. He would be stretched to finance a boat, but there were a lot of old trawlers in the Finnish fleet (the average age of the fleet was twenty-eight years), and he figured he could buy an older one for one hundred-fifty thousand euros or less. Trawlers normally require a crew of two and he would have to hire a first mate. Then he could go into business for himself, fishing for Baltic herring and sprat.

As he thought about his plan, Cecilia's comment at the party at the Hilton Helsinki Kalastajatorppa hotel came back to him. She had said that if he ever got into fishing, he should get a dog to help pull in the catch. A Labrador retriever. Gustave consulted his charts and saw that his filed course was to go south, around the south of Newfoundland. However, if he changed course and went through the Strait of Belle Isle, which separates Labrador and Newfoundland, it would actually be a shorter route to the Gulf of St. Lawrence. It would also take him directly past the village of Red Bay, Labrador. He decided to head for the Strait and stop at Red Bay. Maybe he would be in luck and could acquire a dog there to work with him when he got his fishing trawler.

As Gustave headed into the Strait of Belle Isle, the wind picked up and became a gale. He found his ship enveloped in wisps of fog that streamed past like strands of confetti streamers. The ship began to roll violently from side to side, and Gustave strained to hold a course to the south southwest. His ship struggled against the strong tidal current which was taking him northward off of his course. Intermittent small ice floes now appeared in the water, and swept past the ship. He began to realize why the itinerary had been set to go south around Newfoundland. He consulted the chart again and realized that the Strait of Belle Isle—on the north side of Newfoundland and one hundred twenty-five kilometers long—at that point was very narrow, only fifteen kilometers wide. It was like water pouring through the neck of a bottle. Now the coastline was coming into view through the glass window on the right side of the bridge. Although the view was obstructed by intermittent streams of fog, Gustave could make out huge boulders. He gunned the engine to full power, to try to keep the ship from being swept closer to the coast by the tidal current. In addition to rolling from side to side, the ship was now pitching up and down, with the bow and then the stern alternately rising twenty or more feet above the sea, and then crashing down again and again. Each time the bow crashed down into the oncoming waves, a wall of water would sweep over the deck, coming as much as half way up the side of the bridge, causing Gustave to lurch forward so much that one time he banged his head on the front window. The waves were now coming from the west, and he knew he had to keep the ship headed into them, regardless of the pitch of the ship, since to get even partly sideways to them would be certain to capsize the vessel.

At the same time, the tidal current was proving too much for the ship's engines. The forward speed of the ship had slowed to the point the rudder would not keep it on course. The Viking Libertarian was moving forward, but it was also yawing to the north, taking it closer and closer to the coast. Gustave gritted his teeth and fought the wheel, trying to keep the ship headed into the waves and still moving southwest. He was losing this struggle. As dusk set in, he turned and saw to his right, out the window, the faint outlines of some buildings. The village of Red Bay! His pulse quickened as he saw hope for his situation, if he could only get there before the current pushed him further north.

As the vessel edged closer and closer to the coast, and to the village, Gustave saw what appeared to be a breakwater ahead, just beyond six or seven buildings he could make out on the coast. It was actually Saddle Island, and it shielded the port from the pounding tidal waves. If he could get in the lee of it, he could maneuver and reach the calmer water of the port. He eased the ship past the rugged coastline not more than 300 feet from the rocks, and into the lee of the island. Then he turned the ship to the right, slowed the engine, and eased the vessel into a berth at a waiting dock. Two men came out of the shed at the end of the dock and winched the lines that were thrown to them to four large stanchions. The ship was safe!

Hayden and Darnell, the two men who helped berth the ship, waved their arms for Gustave to disembark the M/S Viking Libertarian.

Gustave threw a rope ladder over the side of the ship and climbed down to the dock.

Hayden yelled at him over the scream of the wind, "You're damn lucky to be here. Nobody goes through that narrow channel on the east side of the island; you have to go on the west side. You must have missed the rocks by only a few feet!"

Gustave hollered back, "The tidal current was too strong; the ship was losing steerageway; there was no way I could get to the west side of the island! You're right, I was lucky to make it through that narrow channel."

At this point about half of the 260 people in the village of Red Bay were at or near the dock, and most of the rest of them were on their way to the dock. Not many ships came to Red Bay anymore, and of those that did, the Viking Libertarian was the largest they had seen in many years.

Gustave asked both men, "How do ships get in and out of here, anyway? And what is the weather forecast? I can stay only a short time; I've got a cargo I have to take down the Seaway."

Darnell responded, "Don't worry, you won't have any trouble. You just need to wait about six hours, and then leave."

Gustave was incredulous. "Six hours! It will be dark then! You want me to leave in the dark and crash up on the rocks so you can loot my ship?" He was getting mad.

"*No, no*" said Darnell. "You really don't understand. You just have to wait for the tide to change. When you came in, it was flowing out toward the Atlantic, against you. In six hours, it will be flowing the other direction, and it will shoot you out of here so fast it will feel like you're riding a rocket!"

The crowd of residents circling around Gustave was all excited and loudly babbling "No, no trouble leaving! You just have to go at the right time!"

Gustave was relieved. Someone invited him to come to the Red Bay Saloon and have a drink. He joined the group moving away from the dock and walked with them up the hill to the small village. The Red Bay Saloon was the most prominent building on the one street of buildings that was Red Bay. It was a lot more impressive inside; there were stuffed caribou heads on each wall and above the long bar. The place was packed with people, at the bar and at numerous tables in the large room. Children ran through the bar chasing each other. Three black dogs lay against the opposite wall, taking it all in. Sawdust and peanut shells littered the floor. The Red Bay Saloon was clearly the community center for the village.

The group inside made a place for him at the bar, and gathered around him as they had at the dock to see this stranger who had arrived at their town. A bottle of Black Horse—brewed across the strait in Newfoundland—appeared before Gustave.

"Here," the bartender announced, "bet you never had a Black Horse! Best beer this side of Quebec!" The man was born in Red Bay and had never been out of Red Bay, but had heard of Quebec.

Gustave took a swallow and agreed. "That's good beer."

He was about to say, have you ever tried a Grolsch? but stopped himself. He did not want to get into an argument with the locals over what was the best beer. Instead, he told them why he had stopped at Red Bay.

After describing his journey, Gustave continued, "I'm going to own my own fishing trawler when I get back to Finland. I'll fish for herring and sprat in the Baltic Sea. I've been told I should get a good Labrador retriever to help me pull in the nets."

The man next to him spoke up, "Whoever said that is right; Labs are strong and love to pull. All the fishermen here use them to pull in the nets. The cold's OK with them, and they're great water dogs. And a good Lab will rescue you if you fall off the boat into the sea!"

Gustave thought that was exactly what he should have. "OK, that's what I'm going to need. Can I see one of those dogs here?"

Hayden spoke up, "Yeah, sure you can." He turned around and called out, "Skaggs! Yip! Yap! Come!"

At that command, the two younger dogs bounded up, dashed over and sat in front of him, tails wagging. The older dog, Skaggs, got up more slowly, ambled over and also sat in front of Hayden, looking up at him.

"These are great dogs," Hayden continued. "Skaggs, here, the old man, taught these young pups to pull nets and all kind of tricks."

Gustave thought a moment, and said, "Would you at all be interested in selling a dog?"

Hayden thought and said, "Well, maybe one of the young ones. I might consider that."

He was silent for a while and then said, both sadly and a bit bitterly, "Fishing is not so big anymore in Red Bay. The waters were overfished, and the government put in new quotas, which make it real difficult to earn a living now-a-days. These are good, smart dogs, and now I don't have enough work for them. A good dog needs a job to do. They're a lot better off when they have something to do, not just lay around. So maybe, I dunno, I might sell Yip or Yap."

Gustave looked at the dogs. He was impressed with Skaggs, and not so much with the other two. Skaggs was a good looking, friendly dog. He could see that Skaggs was strong; his shoulders were broad and powerful, and his haunch muscles rippled under his black coat. He wasn't a young dog, that was for sure. Gustave could see he was white under his muzzle, which made him look like an old man with a white beard. "How old is he?" he asked.

"He's about seven years old. But he has a lot of life left in him, though," Hayden replied.

"You know; I don't think Yip or Yap is the right dog for me. I'd like to buy Skaggs, even though he is older. Then when I can get a younger dog, he can help train it. That's more what I need, an older calm dog just like him."

Gustave was also thinking, Yip and Yap are terrible names; I don't want a dog with a name like that!

Hayden pulled back a bit in reaction to Gustave's statement. "No, no, I couldn't sell Skaggs. He's my best dog, and he's been with me forever. No, I couldn't sell him."

Gustave then said, "Well, he is seven years old, but he looks like he has a few more good years. When I get back to Helsinki, I can get a young dog, and I sure would like him to help train it. I won't have the time or know-how to train a pup, and if I can get a dog that already knows the ropes, so to speak, that would be the best solution. I'll give you $50 for Skaggs."

Hayden slowly responded, "Like I said, we have more dogs here now than we can take care of or feed." Then he repeated, "Skaggs is my best dog."

Gustave said, "I'll give him a really good home. He'll be well taken care of, be assured."

Hayden thought and thought. Gustave looked like a good man to him. He did have more dogs than he needed or could really take care of, and times were hard. Fishing was down, and money was hard to come by. A few men in the village had put their older dogs down, to save money on dog food needed for their younger dogs. Hayden took a deep draw on his Black Horse beer. Then he said, a bit reluctantly, "Make it seventy-five dollars."

A deal was made. Gustave gave Hayden seventy-five dollars Canadian, and promised to give Skaggs a good home for the rest of his life. Hayden gave Skaggs a gruff goodbye, and told him he was now going with Gustave. Then they all had more rounds of Black Horse. When the tide turned, Gustave left with Skaggs and went back to his ship.

Hayden walked home for the first time he had done so without Skaggs at his side, since the dog was a pup. He ate his dinner in silence. As the evening wore on, he thought and thought, oh, what have I done? He missed his dog. He mused about all the good times they had had together. Why did I sell my dog? Maybe I had too many Black Horse beers, he thought. What did I do? Why didn't I see this more clearly? What was I thinking? The life lesson he had just learned hit him like a ton of bricks, like he was buried under it. Never, never, let go of the one who loves you. One who has given you so much. One with whom you have shared so much hard work, and also so much fun and joy. Hayden went to bed and cried. It was a long time before he could sleep.

CHAPTER 5

APRIL FOOLS

Skaggs looked back for Hayden, and clearly missed him. But soon he felt OK with Gustave. He was tired of lying around the Red Bay Saloon, with nothing to do. When Gustave hoisted him onto the deck of the M/S Viking Libertarian, he was glad to be back on a boat. He was accustomed to the roll of a ship, and he liked the cold air and the smell of the sea. Gustave was a seaman, and Skaggs felt at home with him. He didn't have any nets to pull in, so a day after they got under way, Gustave rigged a sheave (a pulley) on the side of the bridge. He put a bucket on one end of a line that went through the sheave and then back down to the deck. When he needed anything brought up to the bridge, he (or Skaggs!) put it in the bucket, and Skaggs pulled on the line and hoisted it up to the bridge. Skaggs quickly learned to give the line a quick yank, causing the bucket to jump a couple of feet in the air, and then just as the bucket started to fall back down he would catch the now slack line a few feet further up and yank it again. By doing this a few times he would quickly lift the bucket the twenty feet or so up to the bridge, where Gustave would retrieve the contents. Gustave could see that Skaggs was a smart dog; he only had to show him once what he wanted and Skaggs got it.

It had been easy to leave Red Bay Harbor. Darnell and the people at the village had been right; the incoming tidal current he rode out was as strong as the outgoing tidal current he had fought so hard to get in.

The Viking Libertarian fairly flew through the Strait of Belle Isle and on into the Gulf of St. Lawrence. Gustave more than made up the time he had spent docked in Red Bay, and because of the shorter route was two days ahead of schedule when he passed Ile d'Orleans and got his first glimpse of Quebec City high on the bluffs above the river on his right. He continued up the St. Lawrence River to Montreal, where the ship passed through the eastern entrance to the St. Lawrence Seaway.

It was good he had gained two days on the scheduled journey, as the Seaway was crowded with ships waiting their turn to pass through the many locks which raise or lower them from one level to another. At the St. Lambert Lock, the eastern-most lock on the seaway, Gustave had to wait six hours to enter. It lifted the Viking Libertarian fifty feet from the level of the Montreal Harbor to that of the Lapraire basin. And so it went as Gustave proceeded through the next five locks on the 431-mile trip through the seaway. The Cote St. Catherine lock lifted his ship 30 feet; the two Beauharnois locks 41 feet, the Dwight D. Eisenhower lock 38 feet, and the Iroquois lock, about 5 feet, to adjust to the level of Lake Ontario. At each lock, he gave Skaggs an envelope containing the lock fee. Skaggs would jump from the deck of the ship to the quay running alongside the canal entrance to the lock and carry the envelope to the lockmaster's office. The lockmaster was invariably impressed that a dog brought the payment to him. After the first time this happened—at the St. Lambert lock—the lockmaster sent a note on his telex to the other lockmasters telling them about Skaggs and the Viking Libertarian. Each lockmaster was so interested in seeing a dog bring him the lock payment that from then on as Gustave approached each succeeding lock, he was waved through to the front of the line. After the Iroquois lock he continued on to the western entrance to the seaway, on Lake Ontario just north of Erie, Pennsylvania. Then the ship entered the Great Lakes-St. Lawrence Water Route which would take it to Lake Erie, and Cleveland, Ohio.

In order to get from Lake Ontario to Lake Erie, the Viking Libertarian had to go through the Welland Canal, a 42 kilometer ship canal from Port Weller, Ontario, to Port Colborne, Ontario, on Lake Erie, which is 99.5 meters higher than Port Weller. The canal enables ships to ascend and descend the Niagara Escarpment and bypass Niagara Falls. Seven lift locks raise or lower ships passing through the canal. The Viking Libertarian entered the canal and passed through Locks 1 and 2 with no delays. However, when it came to Lock 3, there was a line of ships waiting to enter the lock. Gustave got in line alongside the quay and prepared to wait. But shortly thereafter, first one, then another, and another and another of the ships that he had been told by the lockmasters to pass when his ship was traversing the St. Lawrence Seaway locks passed by him, and boxed him in.

As the first one went by, its captain yelled out, "You and that grandfather dog of yours are last this time, buddy!"

Then another of the ships pulled in behind him. He was completely boxed in, unable to move in any direction. But no ships were moving anyway.

Gustave said to Skaggs, "Let's see what's going on here."

He locked the door to the bridge, and they both jumped down to the quay and walked up to the lock. Gustave saw that the first lock door was shut, but as they passed it he also saw that the water in the lock was down, and the door at the other end was open. They walked on, until they came to the lockmaster's office. Gustave asked the lockmaster what was going on.

The lockmaster replied, "One of the pins in the main hinge on the right door failed, and the door was leaking badly. When they looked at it, the other pins looked like they're about to fail also. If that happens, and the door blows out, whatever ship is in there will have quite a ride. It's very dangerous. So they're taking the door down to replace all the pins. It should take about a day and a half."

Gustave said, "Gosh, I'm captain of the Viking Libertarian, the fourth ship back. And there are five others who think they will go before me. When do you think we'll get through?"

The lockmaster looked at his watch, and said, "Today's Monday, March 31; I'd say Wednesday about two o'clock p.m. for your turn. But you ought to be ready early that morning, in case things move faster than I think they will."

Since he had a lot of time on his hands, Gustave decided to see Niagara Falls. He hailed a taxi coming down the Welland Canal Causeway and jumped in the back door when it stopped. Skaggs got in right behind him.

As he shut the door, the driver turned around and said, "Hey, you can't bring a dog in here!"

"Well, he goes with me," said Gustave. "Do you want the fare or not!"

The taxi driver thought—he didn't want to lose the fare—and said, "Well, OK, but I've got to charge extra for him."

"How much?" asked Gustave.

"Fifty dollars."

"That's robbery! How much do you charge for a piece of luggage?"

"Seventy-five cents."

"OK, that's how much I'll pay for Skaggs. Do you want it or not?" Gustave looked like he wasn't going to back down.

The driver, feeling defeated, grumbled and said, "OK, seventy-five cents, but don't tell my dispatcher. Where do you want to go?"

The trip to Niagara Falls was only about nineteen kilometers, and took twenty minutes. The taxi driver drove onto Queen Elizabeth Way to the Niagara Veterans Memorial Highway, and then took Main Street to the Lower Funicular, just below Horseshoe Falls. As they approached the destination, Gustave remarked to the driver that the traffic seemed awfully heavy.

"Yes, it's gotten really bad today," the driver replied. "The City of Niagara Falls on the US side has been in a severe economic decline, and so the mayor and the city council over there came up with this hare-brained idea to drum up more visitors to the falls."

"What's that?" asked Gustave.

"Once a year, on April Fool's day—tomorrow—they allow any damn fool to try to recreate any stupid thing that has ever been done, or any new stupid thing to cross the falls, or go over the falls, or swim up the falls, or whatever. If you stay around tomorrow you're sure to see someone go over the falls in a barrel, and a bunch of other dumb things that get people killed. I think there is even some guy who is going to try to impersonate Evel Knievel and try to jump over the falls on a motorcycle."

When Gustave and Skaggs walked around on the Canadian side of the falls, Gustave talked to lots of people about stunts at the falls. He learned that after Red Hill, Jr. died in 1951 going over the falls in an inner tube barrel, the City of Niagara Falls on the US side banned stunts like that, even though others had done it and lived. In 1901, a sixty-three-year-old school teacher, Annie Edson Taylor had gone over the falls in a barrel with her cat and survived. Annie wasn't the only one—Bobby Leach went over in a steel barrel in 1911 and Jean Lussier in 1928 in a big rubber ball. Both survived. But before Hill's death, Charles Stevens went over the falls in a large, heavy Russian oak barrel, and George Stathakis went over in a 2,000-pound barrel, and both had died. So, when Hill died, the authorities had decided "enough was enough."

That didn't stop people from trying, however. They just had to be a little more discreet in starting out. In 1961, Nathan Boya went over the falls in a steel ball wrapped in rubber, which he called the "Plunge-O-Sphere," survived, and was fined five hundred dollars. David Munday went over in a steel barrel twice, in 1985 and in 1993. Steve Trotter went over the falls in a barrel built from two Greek pickle barrels in 1985, and in 1995 he went over the falls again, with a partner, Lori Martin, this time in a barrel built from two hot water tanks. He was thrown in jail for two weeks and fined five thousand dollars, and Ms. Martin was fined two thousand dollars.

In 1988 two more people went over the falls together in a barrel. Then in 1995, Robert Overacker went over the falls on a jet ski. He had a rocket-propelled parachute strapped to his back, and his plan was to activate it just as he was going over the brink of the falls. He would ditch the Jet Ski and float safely down to the Maid of the Mist pool. However, the parachute didn't deploy, and he fell 180 feet to his death.

Probably the luckiest stunt, by far, was done by Kirk Jones. In 2003 he floated down the Niagara River on his back and went over the falls with no protection whatever. He survived uninjured except for sore ribs. He declined an offer of help from a tour boat at the bottom of the falls, swam to some rocks, and climbed out.

But the event that led to the change of position by the authorities—which also gave some legitimacy to the crazy things which were planned for the next day—was Nik Wallenda walking a 1,800 foot high wire 200 feet above the river, on June 15, 2012. While no one can take away from his accomplishment, it didn't quite rise to the level of wire walking stunts done more than 150 years earlier. A French aerialist, Jean-Francois Gravelet, who called himself the Great Blondin, first traversed Niagara Falls on a high wire, without a safety net, on June 30, 1859. Subsequently, the Great Blondin repeated his feat in more daring fashion: he walked backward one way and returned pushing a wheelbarrow. He somersaulted and back flipped his way across. He crossed carrying a table and a chair. He crossed on stilts and on a bicycle. He carried a stove one time and midway started a fire, cooked an omelet and ate it. And, in perhaps his most famous crossing of Niagara Falls, he carried his manager, Harry Colcord, on his back.

Nik Wallenda's high wire act over Niagara Falls in 2012 was televised by ABC, and it also drew huge crowds. It turned public opinion in favor of stunts. People forgot about the daredevils who had died at Niagara Falls. Stunts were now viewed as a way to draw more tourists to the falls, particularly to the US side to help revive the economy. And so the law was changed: on April Fool's day, anything was legal, and people were free to kill themselves going over the falls any way they wanted to.

Gustave and Skaggs walked around on the Canadian side, looking at the preparations. Since the US side wanted the most publicity, the crossing stunts were to go from the Canadian side across to the US side where the person who (hopefully) made it across would be greeted with fanfare and be interviewed by the mayor and television celebrities. So Gustave looked at the huge ramp which Diablo Conmalo would use the next morning to try to jump across the Niagara River above the falls on his Harley Davidson CVO™ Premium Custom Twin Cam 110 motorcycle. Diablo was walking back and forth in front of the ramp, pumping himself up by beating his arms across his chest.

He yelled out to anyone within ear shot, "I'm the greatest! I'm the greatest! Watch me jump this Harley across those falls! Nine a.m. tomorrow! I'm the greatest!"

Gustave detected that the great Diablo was actually scared to death. He wondered if Diablo would really go through with the jump the next morning.

Further on they came to two people who were each unloading contraptions from their pickup trucks, which they planned to use to go over the falls the next day. One was a cylinder that looked to have been made from whiskey barrels; it obviously was based on old technology that was used in the past by daredevils trying to go over the falls in a barrel. A woman, Meridith Merriman, wanted to recreate Annie Edson Taylor's stunt done in 1901. She even had a cat with her, just like Annie had had.

The other contraption was more high tech. It looked like it was made from three giant inner tubes, such as for the tires on huge trucks used in mining operations, which in fact they were. The daredevil who was unloading them had fastened them together by inflating the first one with the second around the first, and the third around the second, and then inflating the second, and then the third, so they all held each other together. He then tied them together with hemp rope, so they couldn't slip apart. This created a shape that looked a bit like the symbol for an atom, except that the intertwined huge inner tubes were really fat. They were three fat intertwined elliptical surfaces, just like the form electrons take as they speed around the nucleus of an atom. The open space in the center, i.e., the nucleus of the atom shaped contraption, was where the owner, Robert Operheimer, planned to sit when he went over the falls in it. He called his invention the "Atom Ball."

Finally, Gustave and Skaggs came to Rudolfski Nureyfski. He was overseeing the tightening of a steel high wire cable over the falls. He planned to walk across the cable in his ballet shoes, and do a pirouette when he reached the center of the cable, directly over the falls. Gustave struck up a conversation with him and liked the young man. He thought he was really foolhardy, however, to try to cross the falls on a high wire wearing ballet shoes. He asked Rudolfski what he would do if he fell.

Rudolfski replied that if he fell and got swept over the falls he would try to swim to shore. He said, "Kirk Jones went over the falls in nothing but his clothes and was just fine; he just swam to shore when he got to the bottom."

Gustave thought this was really naïve. He explained, "The water going over the falls becomes aerated; the air trapped in the water reduces its buoyancy and will make it difficult for you to stay on the surface. And the water below the falls will be recirculating; the underwater hydraulics can trap you underwater."

Rudolfski thought and said, "Well, you might have a point. Do you have any suggestions as to how I can deal with that problem?"

Gustave hesitated a moment, because he wasn't sure he wanted to get involved, but then said, "I think you should carry a light line, at least 100 feet long, with one end tied around your waist, and the other end tied to an orange float. You can coil it up and stuff the coiled line in your belt. Then if you fall off and are not killed going down the falls, at least there will be a line in the water that someone can pull on to get you out."

Rudolfski thought that was a good idea, and said he would get one.

All the hotels on that side of the falls were high priced, and also full, so Gustave and Skaggs walked across the Rainbow Bridge to the US side and found a run-down, cheap motel for the night. The first daredevil to do his stunt the next morning was Diablo Conmalo. He was so nervous he was shaking, and he didn't even start his cycle until nine-fifteen a.m. He only did it then because he was told that if he didn't go ahead with the stunt, the City of Niagara Falls would come after him to recover the advance money he had received, which he had used to construct the ramp. So he fired up the Harley Davidson CVO™ Premium Custom Twin Cam 110 motorcycle, made it roar and belch smoke a few times, and then starting from as far back from the ramp as he could possibly get, gave it full throttle. The powerful bike leaped forward toward the ramp, gaining incredible speed and then roared up the ramp. Diablo had a microphone into which he was supposed to say how fast he was going for the television audience to hear, but all one could hear was his high pitched scream as he shot off the end of the ramp up into the air and over the falls.

The motorcycle was so powerful and so fast that Diablo not only went over the falls; he went over the landing area on Goat Island on the American side. He was supposed to land on the grassy area on Goat Island next to the east end of Horseshoe Falls. Instead, the motorcycle with Diablo hanging on for dear life landed on top of a school bus that was parked in parking lot #2 just beyond the grassy area. A group of school children had been bused to the area to watch the daredevils, and the buses were all parked in Lot #2. Fortunately, the motorcycle landed on the back end of one of the buses, which was parked parallel to the line of flight of the bike. It skidded across the entire length of the top of the bus and then crashed down the front windshield. When the front wheel hit the hood of the bus, the bike cartwheeled through the air over the hood and came to rest right side up thirty feet or so in front of the bus. Diablo was still in the seat, his teeth chattering.

The mayor ran up accompanied by a television cameraman.

When Diablo realized that he was alive, and saw the mayor, he stood up on the footrests of the bike and shouted, "I'm the greatest!"

Gustave and Skaggs were right there also. They had taken the pedestrian bridge to Goat Island from their cheap motel which was on Buffalo Avenue just across from the island. Gustave remarked to his dog, "He's the greatest alright; the greatest fool I've ever run into. He's the luckiest, also."

Then they walked back to the Observation Tower and took the elevator down to the river level below the falls, where there were a number of Maid of the Mist sightseeing boats. Lots of people wanted to get on the boats that day. The area was jammed with sightseers waiting to see the falls and the daredevils who would be risking their necks. Gustave thought the boat would be a great place from which to watch the remaining stunts. He bought a ticket for the Maid of the Mist boat ride. When Gustave boarded the first available boat, Skaggs walked on right behind him in the rush of people pushing to get on the board. The ticket taker wasn't looking down expecting to see a dog get on his boat, and didn't see him. Skaggs was just overlooked. Most of the passengers scrambled for seats. Gustave didn't want a seat. He and Skaggs stood near the bow so they could get a better view.

Meridith Merriman was the next daredevil. She had put her whiskey barrel boat on the shore about a quarter mile upstream from Horseshoe Falls, on the Canadian side, and at exactly ten a.m. got inside with her cat. She surrounded herself with a bunch of pillows, as had Annie Edson Taylor, and also like Annie, had a friend inflate the barrel to thirty pounds per square inch with a bicycle pump. Then the friend gave the barrel a push, and it floated down the river to the falls.

Meridith went over the falls in a rush. Those on the boats below lost sight of the barrel in the fog of the mist below the falls. About fourteen minutes later, they spotted the barrel floating down the river towards them. One of the boats maneuvered over to it and the mate pulled it close with a grappling hook. He got a rope around it, and four men pulled it onto the boat. They opened the top, and Meridith stood up, flung her arms around the closest man, and gave him a kiss. This image was captured by a dozen or more sightseers with digital cameras, and the kiss appeared on the front page of papers all over the world. Meridith and the man she kissed then of necessity spent so much time together giving interviews about the event, they got to know each other really well, and got married three months later.

The stunt after Meridith was probably the most spectacular of all. Robert Operheimer had taken the Atom Ball upstream from the falls on the Canadian side, but quite a bit further than where Meridith had started. He was about three quarters of a mile from the falls and up a steep slope from the river when he got into the nucleus of the Atom Ball. Then the Ball started rolling down the slope, gaining speed which carried it to the middle of the river after it left the riverbank. Because it was so big—the Atom Ball was a little more than twelve feet in diameter—the wind caught it and pushed it. That day a strong wind was blowing straight down the river, and the combination of the swift current in the river and the strong wind caused the Atom Ball to accelerate its speed as it was propelled down the river. It was going thirty miles an hour or faster when it reached the brink of the falls. It literally shot off the edge of Horseshoe Falls and through the air to the river 50.9 meters (167 feet) below. Its trajectory off the top of the falls carried it about 75 meters beyond the bottom of the falls, and just in front of the Maid of the Mist boat where Gustave and Skaggs were standing at the bow. The Atom Ball bounced when it hit the water. It flew up in the air completely over the boat, coming to rest on the water about 30 meters behind the boat. The Maid of the Mist quickly turned around; the captain gunned the engine and made way to retrieve the Ball. It was hauled up to the deck, and Robert Operheimer climbed out of the nucleus unharmed.

So far, each of the first three daredevils had completed their stunts and lived to be able to tell about it.

The last stunt was the wire walk by the ballet shoe wearing Rudolfski Nureyfski. He started out on the high wire over Horseshoe Falls at noon. He appeared a bit tentative, and seemed to have trouble with the strong wind, but as the walk went on it looked to those below that he was gaining confidence, leaning to his right into the wind a bit, to compensate for its force. The stunt was going well and as he approached the center of the high wire, everyone wondered if he would really attempt a pirouette on the cable in the center of the wire over the middle of the falls. After all, the wind was quite strong and the mist and fog from the falls had to affect his ability to see the cable, which was wet and slippery from the mist. Rudolfski himself had no doubt as to what he was going to do, however. He felt he was in total control. He had leaned into the wind to compensate for its force, and to Rudolfski, balancing against the wind was no different or more difficult than balancing on the wire. So when he was directly in the center of the wire (which he had marked with red paint, so he would know exactly where it was), he did his pirouette. He was perfect! He didn't even lean one way or the other. He did the pirouette en dehors (turning away from the supporting leg). Then, because that had been so easy, he did the pirouette en dedans (turning toward the supporting leg). He felt ecstatic! It had seemed so simple and easy out there on the high wire, even with the wind. On the ballet floor, Rudolfski routinely did double, triple, and occasionally even quadruple pirouettes. So without another thought, he attempted a double pirouette!

The wind had been steady as Rudolfski had made his way across the high wire and as he did his first two pirouettes. But as fortune would have it, at the exact moment he was in the air in the middle of his double pirouette, a huge gust of wind hit him. When he came down, he got one foot on the wire, but his other foot missed, and he fell, with the wire sliding up one leg to his crotch as he fell down toward the wire, and then down the same leg again as he was flipped over and continued to fall down past the wire. As he fell he pointed his toes downward (or rather, given the position he was then in, upward), and the heel of his ballet shoe caught on the wire. Rudolfski was now hanging from the wire by the heel of one shoe, which was barely hooked on the top of the wire. He thought, oh, oh, what now, this doesn't look goo …

And then his shoe came off.

As he was falling through the air to the crest of the falls 200 feet or so below, Rudolfski had the presence of mind to yank the coiled line with the orange float out of the waistband of his pants and toss it. The wind caught it and carried it out and away from the falls just as Rudolfski himself hit the crest of the falls, going about twenty-five miles per hour. Fortunately, he just missed the edge of the underlying rocks, and went into the brink of the falls where the water was curving downward but not yet vertical. This water was moving slightly faster than the current of the river immediately above, and was accelerating as it fell. However, the speed of the water was much slower than the speed Rudolfski was falling when he hit. It slowed him, and before he was carried to the very bottom of the falls he was going the same speed as the water.

The sightseers on the Maid of the Mist boats below the falls saw Rudolfski's two successful pirouettes, and then watched him fall in the midst of attempting a third. Most of them were unaware that he was trying to do a double pirouette; they just saw him fall. In an instant, he was there; then he was falling, and then he disappeared. It was impossible to see the very bottom of the falls, with all the spray, mist and fog, let alone spot a man somewhere in that boiling cauldron of water. Gustave and Skaggs were in the bow of the nearest boat, straining to spot Rudolfski just like everyone else.

All of a sudden, Skaggs woofed.

Gustave looked at what he was focused on, and saw the orange float. He gave Skaggs the command, "Get it!"

Skaggs immediately leaped over the rail of the boat and swam furiously to the orange float. He grabbed it in his mouth, turned around, and started swimming back to the boat. After twenty feet or so, he let loose of the float and turned back, and then grabbed the line further up from the float. He did this four more times, each time swimming with the line a little closer to toward the boat. At this point, everyone on the boat was either on, or trying to get to the rail on that side of the boat to watch. When Skaggs dropped the line and swam back away from the boat a fifth time, he didn't go for the line again. He had seen Rudolfski in the water, and swam to him. Skaggs grabbed the back of Rudolfski's shirt collar in his mouth, and began towing him toward the Maid of the Mist. He was towing Rudolfski so his face was up and out of the water.

As they had done before, with Meridith Merriman, and with Robert Operheimer, the crew of the boat pulled Rudolfski Nureyfski from the water. Then they pulled Skaggs up as well. Rudolfski was shaken, slightly in shock but not seriously hurt. He had a burn from the high wire on his right leg where he had slid down the wire when he fell. He also had an excruciating pain in his crotch, but that was beginning to lessen. Skaggs was the hero of the day. Everyone wanted his picture, and to shake his paw and pet him. Skaggs' picture was also in newspapers and television stories about the Niagara Falls daredevils which ran everywhere that day and the next.

Gustave did not have time, however, to stay around much longer for the news media to interview him and Skaggs. He had a deadline to meet, and he was anxious to get back to the Viking Libertarian and see how the repairs on Lock 3 in the Welland Canal were progressing. He planned to spend that night on the boat, to be ready to move out, if possible, early the next day. After the Maid of the Mist docked, Gustave said goodbye to Rudolfski and wished him well. Rudolfski thanked them both profusely. He gave Skaggs a hug and they parted. In a few moments Gustave and Skaggs faded into the throng of sightseers, and they were celebrities no more. They were just a young man with a sea captain's cap and his dog.

The Maid of the Mist docked on the American side, so Gustave and Skaggs walked across the Rainbow Bridge, for the third time. They were in luck as Gustave was able to hail a taxi that had just discharged its passengers in front of the Daredevil Hall of Fame, which was to their right after they crossed the bridge.

Gustave turned to Skaggs, and told him, "Those fool daredevils will probably be in this hall of fame someday, but you're the real hero."

Gustave was sure Skaggs was smiling as he looked back at him and seemed to nod his head in agreement.

CHAPTER 6

GUS

The repairs to Lock 3 had proceeded more quickly than the lockmaster had anticipated. When Gustave and Skaggs arrived at the lock, ships were already going through it. They ran to the Viking Libertarian, seeing that four of the five ships that had passed them and boxed them in had already left their berths, and were either in or through the lock. The fifth ship, which had berthed behind them, was casting off and preparing to move around the Viking Libertarian to enter the lock. Gustave started the engine, Skaggs pulled in the mooring lines, and the ship began to move, following the other ship into the lock. The lock could hold at least three ships of that size, and traversing the lock with one or more ships reduced the lock fee each would have to pay if it went through alone. So it was important not to delay. As he had done previously, Skaggs carried the envelope with the lock fee in his mouth to the lockmaster's office, and gave it to him.

The trip to Cleveland after leaving the Welland Canal was rocky, but otherwise uneventful. Lake Erie is the shallowest of the great lakes, and can become quite rough in a storm. But the day was sunny and calm, and the Viking Libertarian made the 320 km (198 miles) trip in a little less than twelve hours. Gustave arrived to find the port very busy. The Port of Cleveland was enjoying a renaissance of activity due to an economic boom in Ohio. Manufacturing was returning to the state, and the natural gas industry was booming as a result of the new fracking technology for drilling for oil and gas. The Port had twelve docks in total. The docks west of the Cuyahoga river were for ore and limestone, while the ones on the east side of the river were for general cargo such as imported steel products, which was the cargo of the Viking Libertarian. All of the terminals were full with ships loading or unloading their cargo. Several others were waiting their turn to use the huge cranes for moving cargo on and off of the ships. Gustave moored the Viking Libertarian in the protected harbor behind Voinovich Park, and he and Skaggs went ashore.

The Port had added an extra shift because of the work load, but Gustave learned that it would still be two more days before he could unload his cargo. That gave him an idea. He remembered he had an aunt he had never before met who lived in West Jefferson, Ohio. Aunt Ethelene was his mother Genevieve's sister. She had met a young man from America, Evanar Andersson, who was studying Suomi, the language of Finland, at the University of Helsinki. They had fallen in love, married, and then moved to the United States. Evanar and Ethelene settled in West Jefferson, near Columbus, Ohio. He was smart and creative and worked at home as a fortune cookie writer. She worked as a cath lab technologist at the Ohio State University Hospital in nearby Columbus, assisting in invasive cardiac procedures. Together they raised long-eared rabbits as a hobby. Genevieve had told Gustave many stories about Evanar and Ethelene, and he thought he should take advantage of an opportunity to visit them. He decided to rent a car and drive to West Jefferson. The closest car rental office was Budget Rent-A-Car at 1717 E 9th St., seven-tenths of a mile away. Gustave and Skaggs walked there in less than fifteen minutes.

Gustave entered the office and said to the agent, "I'm Gustave Neiderbaum; I reserved a Ford Focus for pickup here."

The agent looked up at him and replied, "I'm sorry, Mr. Neiderbaum, we don't have any more Focus cars available."

"Well, then, how about some other small car. What do you have for me?"

"The only car we have left is a Ford Flex; it's that one you can see out the window here."

The car he pointed to was a yellow, large, ungainly, boxy vehicle.

"That looks like a small school bus!" Gustave protested. "Look, here is my confirmation number for a Focus. I want a small car that will get good gas mileage like I reserved!"

The agent apologized and said that the last Focus had been leased ten minutes earlier (he didn't admit that he was the one who did it).

Gustave was getting angry. He said, in the calmest voice he could muster, "I must tell you, I'm the captain of the Viking Libertarian, one of the ships of the Nanamamus fleet of ships. When we come to port here, I expect we will just have to give our business to one of your competitors."

At that, the agent looked a bit perplexed. He didn't want to lose future business, let alone this customer. Thinking quickly, he said that to compensate for the mistake he would throw in the insurance damage waiver for free, since the Flex was the only car he had left. But he didn't have any other vehicle to offer.

Gustave still didn't want the Flex, but he had no choice, so he took it. Skaggs jumped in the back and they left for West Jefferson. They arrived late that evening, unexpected. However, once Ethelene and Evanar comprehended who Gustave was, they were overjoyed to see him and Skaggs too. They welcomed them in and the three of them spent the rest of the evening talking about Finland, Gustave's experience at the maritime school at the University of Helsinki, how he met Nanamamus and came to be sea captain of the Viking Libertarian, and about the sea voyage to Cleveland. They listened intently to Gustave's story of the fools who had gone over, or down Horseshoe Falls at Niagara Falls. They were amazed and in awe as Gustave related how Skaggs had saved Rudolfski Nureyfski's life by spotting the orange float and then pulling him out from the bottom of the falls and over to the Maid of the Mist.

Gustave had a good visit with his Aunt Ethelene and Uncle Evanar. She was off-duty the next morning, and fixed a great Finnish breakfast of coffee, open sandwiches with margarine, topped with hard cheese and cold cuts, followed by puuro (porridge) topped with lingonberries and yogurt. After breakfast Evanar offered to show Gustave and

Skaggs his long-eared rabbits. They were in a cage in the back yard. When Evanar, Gustave and Skaggs approached the cage, the rabbits huddled together in the back.

Evanar pointed to the largest rabbit in the cage and announced that its name was "Jack." Gustave thought to himself, gee, that's original, but didn't say anything. Evanar reached into the cage to grab Jack, but Jack moved from side to side avoiding him. After practically getting half of his body into the cage, Evanar was able to grasp the squirming rabbit.

He turned to Gustave and said, "They really seem nervous this morning."

Gustave again thought to himself, of course they are; they're afraid of this big dog here! At that moment, Jack twisted his body in Evanar's hands and escaped his hold. The big rabbit leaped to the ground and took off running as fast as it could around the side of the house. Skaggs took off in hot pursuit.

Evanar yelled, "Stop! Stop!" Then to Gustave, "That dog will kill my champion rabbit!"

Gustave yelled to Skaggs, "Don't hurt it!"

As the rabbit was approaching the street a Ford Mustang driven by a teenage boy was flying up the street, smoke rising from the spinning rear tires as the boy tried to see how fast the car would accelerate. When he was less than a house away, he had to be going at twice the 25 MPH speed limit for that street. The Mustang and Jack were on a collision course. Just as Jack was about to cross the sidewalk headed for the street Skaggs put on a burst of speed and caught up with him. The dog batted Jack with his paw and Jack went tumbling in the grass between the sidewalk and the street, coming to rest no more than twelve inches from the curb as the Mustang roared past. Before Jack could get up, Skaggs picked him up with his mouth around his back. Skaggs carried him back to Gustave and Evanar, and sat in front of Evanar, holding Jack.

Gustave said, "He's saying, 'Here's your rabbit. Take him.' Don't worry, he didn't hurt him. Labs have a soft mouth; they can carry birds and other animals without hurting them at all."

Evanar breathed a sigh of relief, and took Jack from Skaggs' mouth. Then he put the rabbit back in the cage.

After that excitement, everyone went for a walk around downtown West Jefferson. At noon they said their goodbyes. It was a bit sad, because even though they had never met before, in the short time of the visit they had gotten to know each other well. It is a very long way from West Jefferson to Finland, and they all knew, deep down, that it was unlikely they would meet again. Gustave and Skaggs got into the Ford Flex.

As they were about to drive off, Evanar told Gustave, "If you ever find another dog like that that needs a good home, please consider us. He is an amazing dog! I'd give up all of my long-eared rabbits to have a dog like that."

Ethelene agreed, and gave Skaggs a kiss on his cheek.

Meanwhile, in Cleveland, two teenagers, who called themselves "Dirt" and "Devil" (their real names were Robert and Jonathan) decided to steal a car and go for a joy ride. Many people observing them would label them "punks." They had spiked and dyed their hair; Dirt's was purple, and Devil's was red. They had lots of tattoos; Dirt had a skull and crossbones on his forehead, and Devil had daggers on each cheek. Both had tattoos on their neck and arms. Each had a piercing through his nose. They smoked, and threw cigarette butts on the street.

Three years later, after being arrested for much more serious matters than what they were to do that day, a court appointed psychologist would testify that they came from very well-to-do families and were given all sorts of material things, but grew up without structure, rules, discipline, or expectations. He would say they got superficial affection, but not love or meaningful attention. From an early age each had done outrageous things to call attention to himself, such as "mooning" the third grade teacher. Subsequent behavior only got worse. They set off fireworks in the school lockers, and wrote graffiti on walls and cars. The psychologist's diagnosis was that in their youth, each boy was trying, without success, to get his parents' attention. Their absurdly permissive home life and the superficial responses they received from their parents only made matters worse. Later, another psychologist would spin these conditions into a successful defense strategy by saying they were victims of "affluenza."

That day Dirt and Devil had a plan. Although at that moment they clearly looked like punks, the tattoos were fake; they would wash off in a minute with soap and water. The dyed hair also was not permanent; the dye would wash out quickly just with water. Even the piercings were fake. Their plan was to steal a car while looking outrageous, and then later remove the tattoos, hair dye and piercings. They would then not look anything like what a possible witness would remember and describe.

Dirt and Devil had previously noticed an old Chevy Celebrity in a driveway six blocks from Devil's house that had not been moved for a long time. So they went there with a screwdriver and removed the license plates. A few blocks further down they saw an elderly man getting into a Buick LeSabre.

Dirt said to Devil, "Let's get that one!" and they ran to the old man and surrounded him.

Dirt grabbed the old man's arm, and said, "*Ha, Ha, Ha*, I'm Dirt! And he's Devil! Get it? We're the dirt devil! We want your car, old man!"

And Devil said, "That's right, the keys! Quick! Cause if you don't, we'll cover you with devil dirt! *Ha, Ha, Ha!*"

The terrified man handed over the keys to his Buick. Dirt gave him a push backward into some bushes, and he and Devil scrambled into the car and roared away down the street, Devil driving.

They quickly came to a worn looking strip mall. Devil pulled into the parking lot and drove around behind the buildings. It was a deserted area. They got out of the car and removed the license plates from the Buick. They replaced them with the plates they had stolen from the old Chevy Celebrity, and threw the Buick's plates in a trash container. Then they roared back onto the street, and drove until they found a gas station. They parked at the side of the building, used the restroom to clean off the tattoos and hair dye, and then jumped back into the car. They had no place in particular in mind to go, they just wanted to drive around. They figured they could enjoy riding around for a few hours without the car being spotted, since it had different plates, and then ditch it later that afternoon.

After an hour or so, Dirt and Devil found themselves driving west on Chagrin Boulevard towards Interstate 271. Chagrin Boulevard in that area is a main thoroughfare with shops, restaurants, and shopping plazas. They pulled into the Village Square Shopping Center just east of the freeway, looking for a place to eat. After spotting Corkey and Lennie's, a Jewish delicatessen, Devil parked the Buick and they entered the restaurant. Dirt ordered #5, a hot pastrami and corned beef sandwich, and Devil ordered #6, a hot corned beef and chopped liver sandwich. They finished their meal, and left Corkey and Lennie's walking east, looking in the other store windows. They had gone about two hundred feet when they saw a lady with a brown dog leave the Pet People store ahead of them and start across the parking lot. She was carrying a large bag, and from the way she struggled to carry it, they guessed it was a heavy bag of dog food. The dog walked right beside her, without a leash. Dirt and Devil didn't know it, but they were Annabella Rapaski and Buckey, and she had indeed gone to the Pet People store to buy a large bag of dog food. It was "Call of the Wild" salmon, which Buckey loved.

Dirt turned to Devil and said, "Hey, that's a great looking dog! I always wanted a dog like that."

"OK, what are we waiting for?" Devil replied. "Let's go get him!"

But at that moment, Annabella had come to her car, which was a BMW SUV. She opened the back, put the bag she was carrying in the car, and then the dog jumped in.

Dirt turned to Devil and said, "I'll run for the Buick; we'll do the bump and go trick!"

Dirt ran to the Buick which was parked in front of Corkey and Lennie's. Annabella shut the back of the BMW and came around from the back of the car. She went to the driver's door, opened it, and got in. She took her mobile phone out of her purse and then put the purse on the front passenger seat. Then she arranged her hair, fastened the seat belt, and started the engine.

In the meantime, Devil had edged closer to her car, but was hidden from her view by a Ford Explorer SUV parked two spaces from hers. Dirt by then was in the Buick. He backed out of its parking space and whirled the car around and into the lane in the parking lot where Anabella had parked the BMW. As she was backing out of her parking space, Dirt bumped the rear bumper of the BMW with the front of the Buick. Both cars immediately stopped. Annabella and Dirt each got out of their cars to see what damage had occurred.

Annabella was a bit shaken. Her reaction was to apologize, saying, "I'm so sorry; I hope it didn't do much damage to your car. We have insurance, I'm sure they will pay for any damage I caused."

Dirt replied, "Oh, no, it wasn't your fault. It was my fault for bumping your car. You're not hurt, are you?"

Annabella shook her head.

"Let's see what your car looks like," he said. "I want to see if any damage was done to the frame under the bumper."

They both bent down to look at the bumper, and Dirt pretended to look under the bumper. Annabella was bent over watching him. At that moment, Devil slipped into the driver's seat of the BMW, saw that the keys were in the ignition, and started the engine. Fortuitously, the car in the opposing parking space had departed, and Devil gunned the car forward and away from Dirt and Annabella.

Dirt and Annabella both stood up. Annabella was now in shock. She started screaming after the departing car. Dirt turned to Annabella and said, "I saw a policeman over there go into the Pet People store; run over there and report this to him, and I'll try to catch the thief who stole your car!" Annabella was flustered and upset enough not to be thinking clearly, and started for the Pet People store. Dirt ran to the Buick, got in and sped off in the same direction Devil had taken.

While Dirt and Devil had been eating their sandwiches, Gustave and Skaggs were proceeding north on Interstate 71 in the Ford Flex. Gustave had been told to take the I-271 bypass, which he got on just north of Medina, Ohio. By mistake, he passed by I-77, which he should have taken as the most direct route to the Port of Cleveland, and instead continued north on I-271. He was beginning to wonder if he was on the right road when he saw a shopping center ahead at Chagrin Boulevard. He decided to stop and ask directions. He also thought it might be a good place to get something to eat before he turned in the car.

Gustave pulled into the Village Square Shopping Center and was looking for a place to park the Flex, when he saw Dirt run the Buick into the rear of Annabella's BMW. Gustave stopped and watched what happened next. He saw both drivers look at the damage to the cars, and then he saw another person get into the BMW and speed forward. When he saw that, he instinctively accelerated the Flex to the north entrance to the parking lot—which was opposite Corkey and Lenny's—and blocked it, just as Devil arrived at the same point with the BMW. The BMW hit the right side of the Flex and stopped. Devil got out and started to run, leaving the door open.

Gustave and Skaggs jumped out, and Gustave said, "Get him!" At the same time, Buckey jumped out of the open door of the BMW and caught up with Skaggs who was running after Devil. Devil was no match in speed or strength for either dog, and in a moment was on the ground less than fifty feet from the BMW with Skaggs' feet on his chest. Buckey was standing beside him looking him in the face.

Dirt pulled up in the Buick, and saw Devil on the ground with the dogs beside him. He stopped and yelled, "Get in the car!" But that was impossible for Devil. Dirt, even though he was in the Buick, did not react quickly enough to get away. Skaggs jumped up, leaving Buckey to stand over Devil, and stuck his mouth through the open window of the Buick. He grabbed the sleeve of Dirt's shirt in his mouth. While Dirt was struggling to get free, Gustave ran up to the Buick and grabbed Dirt by the neck and yanked him out of the car. Incredibly, Annabella had found a policeman. In a moment everyone was surrounded by police cars, and not much later Dirt and Devil were on their way to the juvenile detention center.

Annabella retrieved her phone and her purse, and called her husband.

"Ralphie," she said, "You won't believe this! Two boys just stole the car and Buckey!"

Anyone watching Ralph would have thought his whole body rocketed two feet in the air as he jumped out of his chair.

"What!" he yelled into the phone. "What happened! Where are you! How did that happen!"

"We're at the mall on Chagrin; we're OK. A sea captain and his dog rescued us. Oh, he's also a gorgeous young man!" And then she told him what had happened.

Ralph said he wanted to meet Gustave and insisted that he and Skaggs come to their home. After the phone call, Annabella did as Ralph said. She persisted in her invitation to Gustave, telling him it was neither far nor out of his way, and that he and Skaggs had to come. After a few minutes of Annabella's persuasive pleas, Gustave agreed, although he really wanted to get back to his ship.

Since both the BMW and the Flex were drivable, he and Skaggs got in the Flex and followed Annabella to her home. Ralph and Annabella lived on Canterbury Lane in Shaker Heights. A golf course was behind many of the houses, and their house was in front of the 14th green. This was both good and bad; it offered a great view, but they also suffered a number of broken windows every year from errant golf balls.

Annabella drove down the street followed by Gustave and Skaggs in the Flex, and then turned into their driveway. Gustave looked up and saw a nice looking gray house. But he quickly saw it was more than just a gray house; it really jumped out at him. The front door was scarlet red and so were the shutters on the sides of the four windows on ground level, and the five windows on the second level. This house was painted to make a statement!

Ralph rushed out of the front door to meet them. He was overjoyed to see Annabella and Buckey. After giving his wife a hug and a kiss, he gave Buckey a pat on his head and told him what a great dog he was. He didn't even look at the damage to the BMW.

Then he turned to Gustave and said, "You must be Gustave, and this is Skaggs. Annabella told me what you both did. I am so glad to meet you. Please come in! There has to be some way I can reward you for your actions and bravery. Many people would not have stopped and gotten involved."

They all went in the house, and Ralph offered Gustave a glass of chocolate milk (Ralph always had a glass of chocolate milk every evening when he came home from work). Gustave accepted the chocolate milk. Then Ralph asked him what he did and where he was headed. As they talked, Ralph learned about the Viking Libertarian and the voyage to Cleveland to deliver drilling equipment, and how Gustave acquired Skaggs, and some of the things Skaggs had done on the trip. When Ralph asked him what he would do when he returned to Finland, Gustave said he wanted to buy his own fishing trawler and fish for sprat and herring in the Baltic Sea. That's why he got Skaggs, he said. He also remarked that when he got back to Finland he wanted to get a strong young Labrador retriever; one Skaggs could train to help pull in the nets.

Ralph thought for a moment and then said, "You know, Gustave, I want to do something to help you. I want to make you an offer. I have a puppy from one of Buckey's litters. I was planning to sell this dog; he is a valuable dog, but I want to give him to you. He is the pick of the litter, which I got because Buckey was the sire. His mother is Abbeygayle Mad River Swimmer; a wonderful dog they call Abbey. This dog is out of Abbey's first litter, and I can tell he will be a great dog. He's just a pup, but he's very strong, curious, gets into everything. He has great potential with the right person and teacher. I'll give him to you if you promise to take good care of him and you and Skaggs give him good training."

Gustave couldn't believe his luck! This was exactly what he wanted for the fishing boat he planned to buy when he got back to Finland. He thanked Ralph profusely, and promised he would do as Ralph asked.

Ralph went to the kennel in the back of the house and came back with a chocolate lab puppy. "Here he is, isn't he a great looking pup!?"

Gustave thought he was the best looking puppy he had ever seen. "He sure is. What is his name?"

Annabella replied, "We call him Wedgewood, because a day after he came here he got the corner of the kitchen tablecloth in his mouth and pulled it off of the table. One of the Wedgewood china tea cups was on the table and it fell on the floor and broke. So we thought that would be a good name for him. But you can call him anything you want."

Ralph jumped in, "Yes, the name going forward will be up to you. Let me get you some papers you can send in later to get him registered with the American Kennel Club after you decide what you want to name him."

Ralph went to his study and came back with an envelope which he gave to Gustave.

"Here," he said, "There's no rush on this, you can send it in at any time. But he's a purebred Lab, so you should get him registered at some point."

Skaggs and the puppy, Wedgewood, were smelling each other. Both were wagging their tails.

Gustave said, "I think they are going to get along well together. I can't thank you enough. Wedgewood is just what I'm going to need, and Skaggs will be a good teacher. But now we must go, because I have to get back to the ship."

As they pulled out of Ralph and Annabella's driveway to head north to the Port of Cleveland, Gustave turned to Skaggs and said, "There's no way I'm going to name this puppy after a tea cup. That's ridiculous! He's going to be a big strong outdoor dog, like you. He needs a good solid Nordic name."

Gustave turned to the puppy and said, "I'm going to name you after me. From now on, your name is 'Gus.'"

Gus, who was sitting on the front seat, looked up at him. To Gustave he seemed to smile. He looked pleased with his new name.

When Gustave and the two dogs arrived at the Port of Cleveland, they found the backlog had cleared and that the Viking Libertarian would be unloaded the next morning. They spent the night on the ship, and the next morning Gustave was busy accounting for the removal of each piece of equipment on the ship's manifest. The consignee—the company to whom the equipment was to be delivered, as well as the customs agent at the port, had to sign off on the delivery. For his part, Gustave obviously did not want to release the equipment until it was paid for. After several hours of negotiation over the bill of lading—the contract between the shipper of the equipment and the ship owner which provides that the ship owner must deliver the equipment to a specific company—the consignee produced a document from the Fifth Third bank, the largest bank in Cleveland. It purported to show that the money to pay for the drilling equipment had been wired to the shipper of the equipment. Gustave thought that was a strange name for a bank. He called the bank to verify that the document was genuine, and then accepted it. This was all quite boring to Skaggs and Gus, who just lay around on the dock and watched Gustave argue with a bunch of other people. But by the end of the morning they were finished. Nanamamus had not arranged for any cargo for the return trip, and so by noon the Viking Libertarian was underway, starting its voyage back to Finland.

Right away bad weather set in, and it would continue for most of the voyage. A gale arose out of the southwest. Gustave was aware that storm winds can alter the lake causing surges that lower it on one side while raising it higher on the other. He knew that Lake Erie can experience storm surges of eight to ten feet. But fortunately the Viking Libertarian was headed northeast, back to Port Colborne, Ontario, at the south end of the Welland Canal. Since the Viking Libertarian was without cargo, it rode high on the water, providing a lot of surface to the southwest wind, which added to the speed of the ship. With the engine at full throttle and the wind pushing, the ship was moving much faster than the waves, which were cresting at seven feet. The ship would rise as it went up a wave and then ride the wave for a few moments before sliding down the trough of the wave. Gustave could feel the ship accelerate as it slid down the trough, and then decelerate as the bow plunged into the water below the wave, only to begin the process again as it climbed the next wave, crested, and rode down its trough. Since the ship's course was almost exactly perpendicular to the waves, Gustave did not need to worry about the ship breeching and possibly capsizing, as long as he kept it that way. He kept his hands on the wheel at all times, constantly adjusting the rudder, to be sure that the ship did not get even the least bit sideways to the waves, which would have been quite dangerous. They made it to Port Colborne in eight hours, two-thirds the time it had taken three days before, going the opposite direction.

They went through the Welland Canal without incident. Skaggs, followed by Gus, delivered the envelope with the lock fee at each lock. Each time after delivering the envelope both dogs quickly returned to the ship and they were soon underway. The trip back through the St. Lawrence Seaway also went smoothly. Gustave debated in his mind whether to chance going through the Strait of Belle Isle again, and decided to do so. He was arriving at the right time for an outgoing tide, and he felt he had handled the following wind and waves on Lake Erie well. With that experience, he thought he could navigate the Strait on an outgoing tide with no problem.

But when they got into the Strait, the wind shifted to the south and dramatically increased in intensity. The tidal current, now flowing northeast up and out of the Strait, was stronger than before, as there was a full moon. The wind, blowing at gale force, was a cross-wind to the ship's course. The full, exposed side of the Viking Libertarian, without cargo, was like a sailboat on a reach, sailing across the wind. This caused it to roll to the port side and as gusts hit the ship, it would roll over so far that Gustave feared water would be on the deck and possibly slosh into the hold. To minimize this meant he had to keep the ship's stern more into the wind, but that put him on a course directly toward the north shore of the Strait. Gustave put the engine into slow reverse, keeping the ship in line with the wind, but also not moving forward. The reverse thrust of the engine counteracted the forward push from the wind. Gustave had to rely on the outgoing tidal current to carry the ship through the Strait, not quite, but almost sideways. This was a unique maneuver, certainly not one taught in maritime school, but it worked! The ship continued to roll quite a bit, but did not get closer to the rocky north shore. And it did get carried through the Strait by the strong tidal current, not very fast, but fast enough to clear the eastern mouth of the Strait before the tide turned.

Through it all Gus was learning his sea legs. And when they entered the North Atlantic he would need them! On the day after leaving the

Strait of Belle Isle the gale out of the south met with a northeaster blowing down from Greenland and Iceland. When the warm air mass coming from the south met the strong cold front of the northeaster, the resulting storm was a cyclone! All around the Viking Libertarian the sky was an ominous gray cover of cloud. As the day went on the wind kept changing direction, as the spiraling winds rotated counter-clockwise. Squall lines followed by thunderstorms periodically streaked toward them and then passed, each time drenching the ship in a driving rain. Occasionally the rain was laced with bits of sleet which bit as they hit Gustave's face whenever he went outside the bridge of the ship to clean the sleet from the windshield wipers on the front windows of the bridge. Throughout these storms, lightning streaked out of the clouds, each bolt followed by a boom that sounded like a cannon shooting at them. This was not sheet lightning followed by rumbling thunder, nor like a huge truck backfiring from its engine braking as it went down a steep mountain. This was like laser warfare with booms magnified by nature's largest amplifier, the ocean itself. With each flash of lightning Gustave counted the seconds to the boom of thunder to judge the distance from the next storm. Later in the afternoon in the distance across the sea to the north he could see a waterspout which seemed to scroll across the surface of the sea like a giant, fat, curved ball point pen; the cloud above being the hand directing it. It stayed to the north of the ship and an hour later disappeared from sight behind them.

Gustave had put Gus and Skaggs in the cabin below where the ship's roll was not as severe, because he was afraid they might be swept overboard. It was anything but a stable place. The ship pitched and rolled the entire time and while they could not see the lightning, they certainly heard the booms of thunder. At first the puppy was uncertain whether to be scared or not. After the first thunderous boom, Gus began to whimper. Skaggs went over next to him and began to lick his coat. Then both dogs lay down together. Gradually the calm of the older dog transferred to Gus as well and as the day went on, he did not even flinch with each succeeding boom of thunder. When Gustave put out their food and water, Gus ate and drank just as Skaggs did, ignoring the instability of the floor on which they were standing and eating. By then Gus had his sea legs, and by the end of the trip he was a true sea dog, able to stand, walk and run on a pitching deck with the best of them.

The storm added another two days to their trip, as Gustave had to reduce speed and constantly adjust course to the wind and waves. But gradually they got to the eastern edge of the storm, and then in a matter of several hours were through it and able to resume course and speed again. They reached the southern edge of the Norwegian Sea and headed south into the North Sea off the east coast of Scotland. Then they proceeded around Denmark and into the Baltic Sea headed for Helsinki.

As Gustave was securing the Viking Libertarian to the wharf in front of the Scandic Hotel Grand Marina, off of Kanavakatu Street in the Port of Helsinki, the ship was met by a steely-eyed bailiff who demanded to come on board. He had with him an arrest warrant which he taped to the door to the bridge. Gustave asked him what was going on. The bailiff introduced himself as Iivari Ilmonen, and announced that the District Court had issued the arrest warrant for the vessel because the Handelsbanken, whose mortgage was in arrears for non-payment, had foreclosed. The vessel was now seized and could not be moved. Iivari also told Gustave that any interference with this process was a criminal offense. The Viking Libertarian would be sold at auction and the proceeds would be used to pay the mortgage.

Gustave was distraught. This meant that Nanamamus had not made his payments to the bank, and probably could no longer be located. The chance of his being paid the second half of his fee for taking the ship with its cargo to Cleveland and back was slim indeed, and his hope of buying a trawler with which to fish the Baltic Sea was evaporating. Without his full pay for the trip, he would not nearly have enough money for a down payment on a boat. The starch went out of him, and he slumped to a chair. Skaggs came up to him and began licking his face. Gus sat at his feet and looked up at him, as though he too realized the dream had slipped away.

Iivari, a few feet away, became quiet, and his stern look melted. Gustave slowly began telling Iivari about Nanamamus and the agreement he had made to be sea captain of the ship for the voyage. He talked about his plan to fish for herring in the Baltic Sea, with his own boat, and started to talk about how that would not now be possible. Iivari listened intently to Gustave. He interrupted after he had the gist of the problem.

"You should consult with a legal advocate," he said. "I'm pretty sure you have a lien against the ship for unpaid wages, which will have priority over the mortgage lien." And Iivari gave Gustave the names of three advocates he thought could help him.

Iivari was right. By law, Gustave did have a lien for his pay, and the bank paid him off so it would not delay an auction of the ship. And the contacts he made at the bank were helpful to him in arranging a loan of his own. After he had his financing in hand, Gustave, with Skaggs and Gus beside him, headed for the fishing docks to find a used trawler he could afford. Gustave's spirits were back, and that transferred to the dogs. Suddenly the sun was shining again! Gustave found a number of boats posted with for sale signs. They were still working fishing boats, but the owners were always ready to sell for a good price. A good sale meant the owner had the chance to move up to a bigger boat.

Gustave found a boat which he guessed to be twenty years or so old, built with a forecastle instead of an aft cabin, which he liked. This style of trawler had a large hold, but less room in the forward cabin than typically in an aft cabin. There was a lot of room on the boat to work the nets. The low gunnels would be an advantage for pulling up the nets, but made working on a slippery deck more dangerous. All in all, Gustave thought this boat, named Beneficial Ringer, was the one for him. The name sounded like good fortune. He estimated what he thought he could catch in a year and what the catch would be worth, and from that determined the top price he would pay for the boat. This impressed the owner, and while both engaged in hard negotiations, a deal was struck. Gustave was about to become the proud owner of the Beneficial Ringer.

That night when Gustave was rummaging through his brief case for the mortgage commitment papers from the Handelsbanken, he found the papers Ralph had given him in Shaker Heights to send in to register Gus with the American Kennel Club. Gustave looked at the papers and realized that most registered dogs have three names, for whatever reason he could not fathom.

He looked at Gus and said, "You are really Skaggs' dog, he has taken care of you, trained you, and taught you everything you know. So his name has to be part of yours."

Then he thought some more, and looked at Gus again and said, "What did Ralph and Annabella call you? Some name after a tea cup, wasn't it? What it was, I can't remember."

He thought a bit more and said, "I think it was 'Westwood' for some kind of china tea cup or something. That's it; we'll name you Skaggs' Westwood Gus." And he filled out the papers to the American Kennel Club to mail the next morning.

But all he ever called Gus was "Gus."

CHAPTER 7

FOURTEEN TONS OF FISH—
AND THEN NO MORE

Almost a year to the day after Gustave purchased the Beneficial Ringer, Eustis Izzielustus found himself ambling down to the fishing docks on the Helsinki waterfront. Eustis was down on his luck. After he had been fired from his job as a dog handler assigned to the crew looking after Bubbling Bedouine he had bounced around from one job to the next, none of them well paying or offering permanent employment.

One job, which he liked the most, was working at the Pet Castle Dog Emporium as a groomer. He got the job because he had worked as a handler at the annual national dog show, but in fact his sole experience as a groomer was only with Labrador retrievers. Labs have a double coat, which is straight and easy to brush out, and giving them a bath and a good brushing is all that is needed. The dogs Eustis was given to groom at the Pet Castle Dog Emporium were something else altogether. His third week on the job, a lady in a flowing, floor length, dyed white reindeer coat brought in her white giant poodle. The dog was given to Eustis to trim and groom.

This dog, which was not well trained and had bad manners anyway, did not like Eustis. When he told it to hold still, it jumped around. It tried to break away and run over to other dogs in the shop. When Eustis grabbed hold of its collar, it whirled around and tried to bite his hand.

Eustis put a muzzle on the poodle, and tied its feet together. Then he got out an electric shaver, and went to work. He shaved the poodle's back, belly, head, legs, and tail, leaving pom-poms around each ankle, its neck, and the end of the poodle's tail. He also left one big circle of hair around the dog's midriff, and he left big eyebrows over each eye. Other than that, the poodle was naked to the skin.

Eustis thought he had done a unique job of trimming the poodle, one that would make it stand out and attract a lot of attention. He was quite proud of himself. He even though the poodle might now have a chance at winning an award at a dog show. The poodle, however, thought otherwise. It was so embarrassed with most of its hair shorn off that it tried to hide under the shop owner's desk. And unfortunately for Eustis, when the lady with the dyed reindeer coat returned and saw her poodle, she threw an apoplectic fit. To mollify her, the owner fired Eustis on the spot.

Eustis' next job didn't have a much better ending. After the pet grooming experience, he finally found work as a window cleaner on commercial buildings. This was outdoor work, and suited him well so long as he was working on only one or two story buildings, which was the case for the first several months. Then his employer got a contract to clean the windows on the Cirrus high-rise apartment building in East Helsinki, which had 28 floors and at 86 meters (282 feet) was the tallest building in Finland. Eustis was suspended by ropes attached to arms protruding from a movable dolly on the roof. As he would finish one window, he would press a key on a remote, and the dolly would move forward as long as he pressed down on the key. Another key would move him the opposite direction. And two other keys would raise or lower him.

Eustis started at the top, and worked down. He was down to the tenth floor, one window away from the edge of the building, and moving to the next and last window on that floor, when an accident occurred at the intersection below. Eustis heard the crash, and looked around to see what had happened, still pushing the key that moved him forward. He was looking at the scene below rather than watching where he was going, when all of a sudden he heard something go "clunk," and then he was swinging in the air beyond the edge of the building. The dolly above had come to the end of its track and bumped into the wall of the parapet on the roof. When it stopped, Eustis, on the end of the ropes, kept moving and swung out beyond the edge of the building. The wind caught him and pushed him out away from the building. He was like a pendulum on the end of a rope 18 stories long.

When he swung back the other way and also back toward the building, he crashed right through the last window on the floor—the one he had not yet washed. Eustis was not hurt, but the elderly man and his wife in the apartment were terrified. They thought they were being attacked. They both screamed and the wife attacked Eustis with a broom. Her husband ran to the phone and dialed 112. Moments later, the Helsinki City Rescue Department arrived. They arrested Eustis and took him out of the building. He was able to avoid a trip to jail because his employer, who had been called by the owner of the building after hearing the complaints of his tenant, arrived on the scene and corroborated his story that he was only a window washer. Nevertheless, he was fired from the job.

Then he answered an ad which was not very specific as to the duties, but promised a lot of pay. Eustis liked that part of it and got talked into working for the company, on commission of course. It turned out to be a telemarketing company and the product, or service, whatever you want to call it, was cemetery lots. Eustis quickly discovered that the only people who really needed a cemetery lot were dead, or almost dead, and they couldn't answer the phone. So he started cold calling all the relatives mentioned in each day's obituaries, in the hope that one of them had the problem of burying the deceased and had not yet purchased a place to put the person. This approach offended about 99% of the people he called. The other 1% already had a cemetery plot for their deceased relative.

After two weeks of making calls, Eustis sold only one cemetery lot. Unfortunately, the sale was not accepted by the cemetery, because the buyer didn't have enough money and his credit wasn't any good. So Eustis was let go. That actually didn't bother him; he hadn't made any money, and didn't like the job anyway. He decided to look for something else to do. Actually, about anything else would be more enjoyable and more promising.

His last job was an apprentice chimney sweep. This was actually a real job, with the promise of advancement. There is a lot of demand, because Section 13 of the Rescue Act in Finland requires owners and businesses to see that fireplaces, smoke flues and ventilation ducts are swept and kept clean on a regular basis. The Ministry of the Interior issued a chimney sweeping decree on August 1, 2005, which proscribed exact regulations on chimney sweeping. A national four-member chimney sweeping qualification committee, nominated by the Finnish National Board of Education, was established to set qualifications for chimney sweeps. Training courses were required to prepare students for the special qualification of master chimney sweep. So the law not only mandated demand for chimney sweeps; it also restricted supply. Since there were less than nine hundred chimney sweeps in the entire country, prices rose, and being a chimney sweep—at least being a master chimney sweep—was a lucrative position.

Eustis got a position as an apprentice, which didn't require prior training; he just had to work under the supervision of a master chimney sweep. The master sweeps got the business, hired apprentices to do the work, didn't pay them all that much, and made a lot of money. Eustis learned the job quickly, and although the work was very dirty and sometimes dangerous, he was satisfied with the job. At least it was a job, he had steady work, and he was making more than he had in his prior jobs.

About six months into the job, he was assigned to sweep the chimneys in a "holiday house." These are houses that are rented out for parties or private use, and the law required that the fireplaces and flues of a holiday house and its sauna be swept regularly every year. Eustis was given the address of the holiday house he was to sweep, and when he arrived got out his ladder and climbed up on the roof. He lowered himself down the chimney, sweeping it as he descended. As he neared the bottom, he slipped and fell into the fireplace in a cloud of soot. He must have appeared down the chimney like a very dirty Santa Claus. Except it wasn't the living room he appeared in; it was the *sauna*. And on the cedar benches all around the small room were naked ladies, each with a glass of wine, taking in the dry heat! Eustis, covered with soot and grime, had rudely interrupted their "sauna party." Mass screaming ensued, as the ladies snatched towels to cover themselves. Wine spilled on the cedar floor, and more than one wine glass slipped from a hand and fell to the floor and shattered. That caused the ladies to jump onto the benches to avoid stepping on shards of broken glass, and more screaming. Eustis spotted the door to the sauna and made a quick exit. The ensuing complaints, however, cost him this job too.

So when Eustis ambled down to the fishing docks at the Helsinki waterfront that day, he was not feeling very upbeat at all. He had been looking for another job for several weeks now, without success. Every place he applied wanted to know where he had worked before, and why he had left. As soon as they learned that he had been fired from his last five jobs, each terminated the interview. Being fired five times wasn't a very good record. As Eustis walked past the fishing boats in their berths, he spotted a hand painted sign in front of one. It read, "Deck hand wanted. Apply to Captain Gustave Neiderbaum on Beneficial Ringer." His first thought was to just walk on past; he didn't want to hear another rejection, and so that's what he did.

Gustave had had a good year. Gus was no longer a puppy; he was now a full grown dog, with a strong broad chest, and strong legs. Skaggs had taught him to help pull in the nets full of herring and sprat, and all three of them had worked hard the entire year. Gustave and the dogs worked six days every week. They were working more days, and longer hours, than any of the other fishermen. It helped that the fish were plentiful and that there had been no major prolonged storms. All of this had enabled Gustave to exceed his estimated catch for the year. And the demand for the fish was up, and so were prices. So the money he had left after mortgage payments to the Handelsbanken and for fuel, maintenance and living expenses was more than he had hoped for. Another two or three years of such luck would allow him to pay off the mortgage on the Beneficial Ringer.

Gustave knew, however, that the Beneficial Ringer was definitely not as efficient as some of the other trawlers. It was a stern trawler, meaning that the trawl, or net, was deployed and retrieved from the stern. However, it had only one drum winch with which to pull in the net. This meant that the horizontal opening of the net below the surface of the water was relatively small. In order to widen the "mouth" of the net, Gustave had rigged lines from each side of the opening of the net. These lines ran through blocks (pulleys) at the end of outriggers he constructed on each side of the boat, and from there the lines ran into the boat. The boat was unique; Gustave had made it into sort of a hybrid; a combination of a stern trawler (the most common type), and an outrigger trawler. Skaggs and Gus handled the lines from the outriggers, one dog on each side of the boat. This was very important to landing all the fish caught in the net. Each dog had to pull in the line on his side of the boat slightly faster than the winch pulled in the main body of the net; if either side lagged behind, fish could spill out of the net. When everything worked right, the two sides of the net closed together in front of the net, and all the fish were pulled onto the deck of the boat by the winch.

The Beneficial Ringer had a relatively large hold, for its size, but it lacked freezers. Instead, Gustave had to carry ice in the hold below, and pack the catch of fish as it came out of the net into boxes along with ice. He did this work himself, as well as running the boat. He was able to do this as long as the weather was no worse than moderate, but in a high sea, running the boat took all of his attention and storage of the catch had to wait for later. Gustave knew that he really needed a deckhand to help, but until he had made some money he had not wanted to take on the added expense. Now he felt he could, and that is why he put out the sign that Eustis noticed and then passed by.

When Eustis reached the end of the dock, he turned around and started to walk back. This took him past Gustave's sign again. This time he thought, oh, why not. I might as well give it a go, and he looked around to try to find the Beneficial Ringer. Actually, it was right in front of the sign. Eustis saw the name on the stern, and called out, "Captain Neiderbaum!" Gustave came out of the fo'c'sle followed by Skaggs and Gus.

"Hi," Eustis called out, mustering a big smile, "I'm Eustis Izzielustus. I saw your sign and want to apply for the deckhand job."

Gustave and Eustis sat down together on a bench, and Gustave queried him about why he wanted the job and what he had done before. He thought Eustis looked strong enough to be a deckhand, and packing fish in ice wasn't all that difficult. As he talked and described the job his mind started thinking ahead, to finding someone who had the potential to do a lot more, someone who could learn the trade and maybe even eventually take over running a trawler. In the back of his mind he was already thinking ahead to the day he might acquire another boat and do pair trawling, where two boats operate together towing a single, huge trawl net. Then he caught himself, quickly putting that thought out of his head. He snapped back to concentrating on his immediate need: a deckhand to pack fish in ice, and started asking probing questions to learn more about Eustis.

Gustave was concerned about the five consecutive firings, but did not immediately stop the interview when he learned about them as had other prospective employers who interviewed Eustis. Gustave probed the circumstances of each situation that led to Eustis being fired and concluded that Eustis didn't have any real faults, but that he had had a streak of terrible luck. Eustis was like Joe Btfsplk in the cartoon strip Li'l Abner, well-meaning but dogged by bad luck. In the comic strip, a small dark rain cloud perpetually hovered over Joe Btfsplk's head. Eustis was like Joe, only in real life. The problem with Joe Btfsplk was that his bad luck spilled onto everyone who came in contact with him; he brought disastrous misfortune to everyone around him. Fortunately for Eustis, Gustave did not read the comic pages, and was not familiar with Li'l Abner. He had never heard of Joe Btfsplk. If he had, he probably would have said, sorry, Eustis, I don't think I can hire you. The parallel with Joe Btfsplk was too great.

Instead, Gustave asked Eustis to wait a few minutes and left the quay where they were sitting to go to the fo'c'sle cabin of the Beneficial Ringer. He beckoned to Skaggs and Gus to follow him.

When he was inside the cabin, he turned to his two dogs, and said, "What do you guys think of Eustis? Could you work with him? Do you think he would be a good worker?"

Now, Gustave did not really expect an answer. He knew dogs can't talk. By talking to his dogs, he was really talking to himself, asking himself the basic questions that he had to answer. Namely, if I hire Eustis, will we all get along together on a small boat for extended periods of time, and will he be a hard worker?

Skaggs and Gus may not have been able to talk, but each dog keenly picked up on Gustave's mood and feelings. They could sense his troubled indecisiveness about Eustis. On one hand, Gustave saw positive attributes in Eustis' failures; attributes Eustis himself didn't recognize. Eustis was comfortable with dogs, and he would be working with two dogs on the boat. He had worked without panicking in dangerous conditions—washing windows on a high rise building and cleaning chimneys, and packing fish on a slippery deck certainly could be dangerous. And he had shown initiative in coming up with an approach to selling cemetery lots, even if it didn't work very well. Gustave needed a helper who would exercise initiative in getting things done. He had too much to do himself without having to give a lot of instructions to a deckhand. On the other hand, Eustis had been fired from each of his last five jobs.

Skaggs reacted to Gustave first; giving a loud "Arf, Arf!"

Then Gus did the same, "Arf."

That was all Gustave needed. He decided to give Eustis a chance and offer him a job on the Beneficial Ringer. He felt the dogs had accepted Eustis, and he was coming around in his thinking that all Eustis really needed was encouragement to focus on the job all the time, and not get distracted. That was what had led to his misfortune. The way the dogs worked on the boat as well as himself would set a good example for Eustis. He returned to the bench on the quay and offered Eustis the job. Eustis was ecstatic that he had been given another chance. He enthusiastically accepted Gustave's offer.

Gustave was planning to head out to sea the next morning, and so they spent the rest of the day getting supplies on board. They needed food for at least twelve days and lots of boxes for packing fish. Eustis lifted the boxes from the quay to the deck of the boat. Skaggs and Gus pushed them over to the hatch to the hold, and Gustave stowed them below. They got the ice last, moving big bags of ice the same way. Gus liked pushing ice bags best of all. He kept nudging Skaggs out of the way and ended up pushing most of the ice bags himself. Gustave filled the ice locker in the hold and the ice chests next to the fo'c'sle to the top with bags of ice.

The next morning Eustis met the boat at 6:00 a.m. as requested and they cast off. Gustave's plan was to steam north on the Baltic sea into the Gulf of Bothnia to a point about opposite the town of Vaasa on the Finnish coast, which is a little more than halfway between Helsinki and Oulu. From there he would begin trawling, working his way further north.

About one hundred kilometers (sixty-two miles) north of Aland Island, in the Gulf of Bothnia opposite the town of Pori, they passed the spot where a mysterious disc shaped UFO about sixty feet in diameter had been discovered on the bottom of the sea by a Swedish ocean exploration team. According to the Swedish Ocean X Team who had looked at it, the object appeared like a huge mushroom, sixty feet across and rising ten to thirteen feet from the seabed, with an extremely smooth, rock-like surface. It had rounded sides and rugged edges, and an egg shaped hole leading into it from the top, as an opening. It also had strange stone circle formations on the top, almost looking like small fireplaces. The stones were covered in something resembling soot. The disc itself was at the end of a 985-foot-long path in the sea floor that looked like a runway.

Gustave had read about the mysterious disc and knew where it was located, but to him it was just one of the mysteries of the Baltic, and one which did not concern him. Gustave did not worry about UFOs. What he did worry about is the fact that the Gulf of Bothnia north of the Baltic Sea is the largest body of brackish water in the world, and usually about 45% of it freezes over. Offshore, the ice is dynamic all year, and is easily moved about by the wind, which meant that he had to constantly be on the lookout for ice floes. Also, he had to be aware of the salinity of the water he fished. Because of the huge amount of fresh water that flows into the Baltic Sea from rivers and glaciers, its salinity is much lower than that of ocean water. The salt content is least near the surface and in the northern portions of the sea, and considerably more at greater depths and nearer the Danish Straits. Since the salinity tolerance of herring is between 6% and about 40%, Gustave could expect to find herring in the southern to mid-portion of the Baltic, away from bays with major freshwater inflows.

Eustis listened to Gustave talk about the danger of ice floes, the need to understand the salinity of the sea at different places and depths, and finally about the mysterious disc shaped UFO that had been discovered on the seabed. He had no interest in the ice floes—he hadn't seen one yet—or the salinity of the sea water. But he was all ears about the disc shaped UFO.

He asked Gustave, "When was it discovered?"

"June 19, 2011."

"How deep is it?"

"I think they said 285 feet."

"Who found it?"

"Some Swedish sea treasure hunters."

"Have they found anything else?"

"Yes, they found a ship loaded with 2,500 bottles of champagne."

"How many divers went down to look at it?"

"I only read about one."

"Did they take any photos?"

"I think they did."

"Does it look like a spaceship?"

"I dunno, I think some people think it does. I've never seen a spaceship."

"How old is it? Did they see any aliens? Has it moved since they found it? "Are you afraid aliens from the disc will come after us when we fish in these waters?"

At this one Gustave said, "No! Now shut up!"

Eustis stopped asking questions, but sat in his chair in the fo'c'sle thinking about aliens from the disc. He thought, if they flew to the sea bottom landing strip on the disc, they could probably fly out the same way. Skaggs and Gus lay on the floor pretending to sleep through all this, occasionally opening one eye to look at Gustave, but always keeping one ear semi-cocked so as to hear the conversation.

Gus was now a full grown dog, but he still had the exuberance and playfulness of a puppy. He and Skaggs were communicating in their own way about Eustis. They sensed that he was in a high state of anxiety, but they also sensed that Gustave thought it was ridiculous. Gus decided to play a practical joke on Eustis, and enlisted Skaggs in his prank. Later, after Eustis had gone to sleep in his bunk, the two dogs got on either side of him. Then, both breathing into his face, each thumped a paw on his chest. When Eustis woke with a start, they hid from sight under his bunk. Eustis, who had been dreaming about aliens, was sure he had been abducted by them.

He began pleading for his life, whimpering, "Please don't kill me! Take me back to earth, please! I'll do anything you want!"

After a few moments, now wide awake, he looked around and saw he was in his bunk, by himself. Then he heard the dogs under his bunk. The sound they made sounded remarkably like laughter, if dogs could laugh.

A day later they came to the spot where Gustave wanted to start trawling. He and Eustis spread out the big trawl. It was a large cone shaped net, with a closed end where most of the fish are gathered, and a much larger open end—the "mouth" of the net. There was a float line along the top of the mouth, and a weighted line along its bottom, to keep the mouth open from top to bottom. It also had lines from each side of the mouth to the outrigger arms, to keep the mouth wide open. Gustave showed Eustis how to attach the main cable from the mouth of the trawl to the winch that would be used to pull in the trawl when it was full of fish. He then went up to the fo'c'sle to start moving the boat forward, and called back to Eustis to throw the net into the water. As Eustis moved to the stern of the boat and began picking up the net, his right foot scuffed under a loop in one of the lines from the side of the net that led to one of the outriggers. Then when he turned around to grab more of the big net, the line wrapped around his leg. When Eustis threw the net over the stern, Gustave powered up the engine, moving the boat forward to straighten out the lines from the net. Eustis, with the line from the net tangled around his leg, was yanked over the low gunwale at the stern. One moment he was there, on the boat, and the next moment he was nowhere to be seen!

Gus saw it all happen. He barked and then jumped into the water and began swimming toward the trawl. Skaggs saw Gus jump overboard and immediately ran to Gustave, barking frantically. Gustave looked back and saw Gus swimming toward the trawl, which was now trailing behind the boat and starting to sink into the water. This was because the weights at the bottom of the mouth of the trawl and the floats at its top were designed to take it down to a depth of about 100 feet. Gustave then saw Eustis tangled in the line from the side of the trawl and being dragged behind the trawl. He was in immediate danger of being pulled below the surface of the water as the trawl sank. Gus reached Eustis and grabbed his shirt in his mouth, all the while paddling madly to hold him up. Gustave immediately threw the engine into reverse, closing the gap between the boat and net. The tension on the line tangled around Eustis released when Gustave stopped the boat from moving forward by putting it in reverse. Eustis took a deep breath, put his head under water and reached down to untangle the line from his leg. Then he popped back up and Gus' paddling started moving them toward the boat. In the meantime, Skaggs had jumped overboard with a rope in his mouth and was swimming toward them. Eustis grabbed it; Gustave got the other end and with Gus furiously paddling and Gustave pulling it was a matter of seconds before Eustis was at the stern. Gustave used the rope to pull him on board. He lowered the rope to Skaggs, who grabbed it in his mouth and Gustave pulled him up, and then repeated the effort with Gus.

Eustis was cold and shivering, but OK. He warmed up in the fo'c'sle and put on dry clothes. Gus was the hero of the day. They did not stop to celebrate however; the trawl was in the water and Gustave started the boat forward again to trawl for fish. He could tell from the resistance created when the trawl was full, which did not take long. Then the process of pulling it up, unloading it, and packing the fish in ice began. As the winch pulled up the main body of the trawl, the two dogs pulled in the lines from the outriggers, closing the mouth of the trawl. All of them then helped pull the heavy bag of fish over the stern gunwale onto the deck. Eustis had not had much time to rest after being rescued. The trawl full of fish was dumped on the deck, and he had the job of picking them up and packing them in boxes with ice. One layer of fish, one layer of ice, and so on and so on. In the meantime, Gustave had the trawl back in the water for the second time. Eustis was barely finished packing fish from the first trawl when they were ready to pull it up again and dump more fish on the deck. This went on all day, with only a half hour stop for lunch and another for some dinner. When they finished at 8:00 p.m., they had worked 12 hours that day.

It had not been an auspicious start for Eustis. Bad luck—if it was luck—was still following him around, as it did Joe Btfsplk. Maybe, Gustave thought, the problem was that he didn't pay enough attention to what was around him. Gustave was pleased with his hard work packing the fish, but also concerned about his safety on the boat. It could affect all of them. Thinking to himself, he turned to Gus. Gustave often talked to his dogs as though they could understand what he was saying. It helped him sort out his thoughts to have at least the appearance of talking a problem over with someone else. The young dog had proved he was a valuable member of the team. He had worked hard helping to pack the boat with supplies. He handled his line superbly, all day long. Above all, he had reacted incredibly fast and had rescued Eustis. If he hadn't acted as quickly as he had, Eustis would have drowned.

Gustave said to Gus, "Gus, I want you to watch Eustis all the time. Make sure he doesn't get into any more trouble." Gustave hoped it could be as simple as that, but he didn't expect Gus to understand. Obviously, Gus couldn't answer back. But the way he looked up at Gustave clearly showed he had been listening.

On this trip they did in five days what previously had taken eight. The hold was full with boxes of fish. Gustave turned the boat around and headed south, back to Helsinki. The round trip took nine days, and they were just about out of provisions and fuel when they returned. They unloaded the boxes of fish, which Gustave sold to a wholesaler. Then they got more provisions for the boat, set off, and began the same process all over again.

The Beneficial Ringer, loaded anew with supplies, worked its way north again. Each day the backbreaking work of setting the trawl, then pulling it in, and packing the fish continued, adding more boxes of fish in ice to the growing stack of boxes in the hold. Eustis worked as hard as the rest. He had a couple of close calls. One time he slipped on the deck which was covered with fish scales and ice and almost went over the stern gunwale. An alert Gus grabbed him by the pant leg and pulled him back. Another time in rough seas a wave almost knocked him overboard. Gus saved him that time also. Gustave did note that Gus seemed to be around him most of the time, and no serious accidents happened. Overall, Gustave was pleased; having Eustis pack fish clearly sped up the process.

They did this for the next two years. On the night of May 13 of the second year, they were trawling for herring in the Gulf of Bothnia in the Baltic Sea, about halfway between the towns of Pori and Vaasa on the Finnish coast. Just beyond sight, but not more than five kilometers away, a small cruise ship, the M/S Latvia, was headed north in the Baltic Sea. The M/S Latvia was on its way to the town of Kemi, which is on the north coast of the Gulf of Bothnia, about eighty kilometers from the Arctic Circle.

The M/S Latvia was the only cruise ship to schedule a stop in Kemi. Kemi is somewhat difficult and dangerous to get to by boat because of the ice, even though an icebreaker, the Sampo, is berthed near Kemi and regularly breaks ice in the Gulf of Bothnia. However, the M/S Latvia arrived at port in Kemi the next morning without incident. A young couple, Febber and Glendaloca Rabberace, disembarked with the rest of the twenty-eight passengers. They were on holiday, and had boarded the M/S Latvia in Helsinki. They, like all of the other passengers, were going to visit the Arctic Comic Festival and also see the world's largest snow castle, which is rebuilt each year with different architecture. Febber and Glendaloca also had tickets for a ride on the Sampo icebreaker.

After leaving the M/S Latvia, they headed for the Arctic Comics Center on Keskuspuistonkatu Street about four blocks from the harbor. The festival which started in 1981 is international in scope and as in the past, this one attracted illustrators, critics, researchers and spectators from all over the world. Once inside, they saw many people dressed up as their favorite comic. In addition to Nordic comic characters, which predominated, there was Lucy and Charlie Brown from Peanuts, Dagwood and Blondie, Judge Parker and Katherine, G-I Joe, Little Orphan Annie with Daddy Warbucks and Sandy the dog, and all the superheroes and mystery men including Superman, Batman and Robin, Green Arrow, the Japanese Beetle, Spiderman and Iron Man.

This particular Sandy the dog was actually a very large Airedale terrier.

Glendaloca asked if she could pet Sandy, and Annie replied, "Yes, of course you can. Sandy is a very friendly dog."

Glendaloca had barely turned around to face the dog when Sandy jumped up on her, putting both paws on Glendaloca's shoulders. Then Sandy began licking her face.

"I don't need my face washed, thank you very much!" Glendaloca exclaimed, trying to push Sandy away.

Febber yelled, "Sandy, get off my wife!"

Sandy jumped down from Glendaloca's shoulders and turned to Febber. Sandy wrapped his front legs around Febber and began humping him.

"Sandy, stop! Get off!!" screamed Febber.

Annie, holding back a laugh, because it did look sort of funny, said, "OK, Sandy, leave the nice man alone."

Sandy kept humping Febber.

Annie said it again, "That's enough, you're a good doggie, let the man go now."

Sandy kept on humping Febber, who was trying to get away but wasn't strong enough to pull away from a 110-pound dog who had his front legs wrapped around him.

Just then Spiderman, who was swinging around the room on several ropes which he had earlier tied to eye-hooks in the ceiling, came swinging by yelling, "I'll save you!"

He bent down as he swung by Sandy and grabbed hold of his ear. Sandy let out a loud yelp of pain as his ear was pulled, and let go of Febber.

Daddy Warbucks yelled at Spiderman who was now swinging away in the other direction, "How dare you hurt my dog! You come back here, I'll show you how it feels to have your ears pulled, you miserable insect!!"

When Sandy loosened his grasp, Febber broke free and turned quickly to Glendaloca, saying, "Let's get out of here!"

Both of them ran to the ballroom which was the next room down the hall, leaving Annie and Daddy Warbucks to deal with Spiderman.

This was the first year that the Arctic Comics Festival established a Comics Hall of Fame, and the announcement of the first comic author selected for induction into the Hall of Fame was just getting underway on the stage in the ballroom. When Febber and Glendaloca entered the room, the judges were making preliminary remarks before announcing their decision. There was a burst of applause when they disclosed the name of the first inductee. It was Al Capp, creator of Li'l Abner. Al Capp is recognized by about everyone as the creator of the greatest comic strip of all time. To celebrate his selection and achievements, all of the Li'l Abner characters were there in the room: Li'l Abner, Daisy Mae, Mammy and Pappy Yokum, the Shmoo, Fearless Fosdick, and others. Even Joe Btfsplk was there. The female characters drew the most attention: Daisy Mae, Sadie Hawkins, Moonbeam McSwine, Wolf Gal, and of course Stupefyin' Jones. However, she was not on the stage; she was over on one side of the room stupefying a gaggle of mostly older men vying for her attention. When Glendaloca saw Stupefyin' Jones with the group of men around her, she quickly hustled Febber to the opposite side of the room, to prevent any chance of *him* being stupefied.

After looking at comic strip exhibits in each of the other rooms, Febber and Glendaloca went to see the SnowCastle, which is the biggest snow castle in the world. It covers up to 20,000 square meters and is three stories high. Inside is the SnowRestaurant with ice tables and seats covered with reindeer fur. That afternoon they said their marriage vows again in the SnowChapel, and then they had dinner in the SnowRestaurant. After a dinner of cream of reindeer soup with cheese, roasted salmon with herbs, dried herring, and wild berry sorbet for dessert, they went to the SnowHotel for the night. Febber had made a reservation almost a year earlier for the honeymoon suite (the SnowHotel always sells out months in advance as there are only 18 double rooms, two group rooms, and the honeymoon suite). They had a drink at the CastleLounge, and then went to their room in the SnowHotel for the night.

The bed in the honeymoon suite was toasty warm and they slept well, even though the temperature throughout the hotel is only -4.5 centigrade. The next morning Febber woke up first and jumped out of bed to start the coffee pot.

As he was in mid-air between the bed and the floor, Glendaloca screamed at him, "Get your slip…" and then Febber's bare feet hit the floor.

Glendaloca finished the sentence, "Get your slippers! Don't forget to put on those slippers they gave you before you get out of bed!"

The slippers she was yelling to him about had been given to them at the front desk the night before, and the clerk had warned them to always put them on when they got out of bed. The slippers had insulating soles about an inch thick, with sandpaper bottoms. The purpose of the slippers was so their warm feet—they were sleeping in a bed with an electric blanket—would not melt a glaze of ice on the ice floor, which would then instantly freeze, causing them to be stuck to the floor. The slippers also assured they would not slip on the ice floor. Febber unfortunately had forgotten the warning. When his feet hit the ice floor, he immediately stuck to the floor. One foot was in front of him, and the other behind him, with his knee bent.

"Help! Help!!" He screamed. "I'm stuck!!!!" Febber was stuck just like Ralphie's friend Flick's tongue was stuck to a frozen flagpole in the movie *A Christmas Story*.

Glendaloca grabbed her slippers and crammed her feet into them. Then she ran for the door yelling for help. Six guests in other rooms poked their heads into the snow hallway.

Glendaloca called out to them, "Help! My husband's feet are stuck to the ice floor!"

In a moment, all six were running to Febber and Glendaloca's room to try to help Febber get unstuck. One brought a carafe of hot coffee, another a pot of hot chocolate. A third brought a bottle of vodka, and a fourth brought a hair dryer. A fifth brought an ice pick and the sixth brought a gasoline powered chain saw. When Glendaloca saw the ice pick and the chain saw, she about fainted.

"You can't cut off his feet!" she exclaimed.

When they all got to the room, they tried the hot coffee and hot chocolate first, but the liquid just ran out on the ice floor, where it froze. They tried the hair dryer next, one foot at a time. Febber yelled that it was too hot on the top of his foot, so they moved the hair dryer a little to the side to try to melt the ice under his foot. This just seemed to melt a little of the ice, and as had happened with the coffee and hot chocolate, the water from the melted ice simply ran out on the floor and froze again. So then they poured the vodka around and over each foot. That helped; it was like antifreeze. The water with all that alcohol in it couldn't freeze. But it still ran out on the floor, away from his feet.

In the end, they had to use all six of the items to free Febber. The man with the chainsaw cut a notch all around each of Febber's feet—as Febber held one arm over his eyes, afraid to look. Another chipped some of the ice out from under his feet with the ice pick. Then as the ice melted from the coffee and hot chocolate, it stayed in the depressions around each foot, and it didn't refreeze because of the vodka mixed in it. They used the hairdryer to keep the brown liquid surrounding Febber's feet hot. It soon permeated all the way under his feet, and then Febber was free! Glendaloca told him to put on his slippers and take a hot bath. The water for the bath was geothermally heated and Febber quickly thawed out and was ready for the next activity.

That was a ride on the Sampo Icebreaker, which they had to board between 11:30 a.m. and noon. The Sampo is based in Ajos, 12 kilometers south of Kemi, and they had tickets for the snowmobile safari to get there. They went to the Safari House, a short walk from the SnowHotel, and changed into snowmobile suits, wool socks, boots, mittens and helmets. Each person on the safari had to drive a snowmobile first over the frozen tundra, and then over the frozen sea, where the ice had become jagged and craggy from the effects of the wind. It was a bumpy and somewhat dangerous ride, but no one tipped over or fell off his or her snowmobile. They met the Sampo in the midst of frozen sea, where it was waiting for them.

The Sampo was a very interesting experience. They stood on the deck with the other passengers watching the ship break through two-foot-thick ice, which created huge blocks of floating ice in the wake of the ship. Then they took a 30-minute tour of the entire ship, including the engine room, and the captain's bridge. Lunch was served in two settings due to the limited capacity of the restaurant on board the Sampo. Glendaloca had the cream of salmon soup and Febber chose the cream of reindeer soup. Cheese, bread, butter and drinks were included in the price. The restaurant even offered a vegetarian lunch which was chosen by a few of the passengers.

The next activity was the plunge into the icy Baltic for swimming or floating while dressed in impermeable survival suits. Since there were more passengers than suits, the passengers had to take turns. Almost everyone participated and in turn put on one of the 20 impermeable survival suits. However, one lady refused to get into the suit she was given because she thought it was "unhygienic." Actually she was right— the suit reeked of body odor. The previous passenger who had used that suit was a somewhat overweight lady, and the neoprene rubber suit was too tight for her and had caused her to overheat and sweat profusely. In addition, she had had the vegetarian lunch, which featured lovage soup—lovage is also called "smallage" and "smellage"—which caused her to fart multiple times while she was in the suit. The sweat and the farts combined to create one awful smell. That suit was next offered to Febber. He and Glendaloca were the last two guests in line, and so the choice was either to take it, or miss the swim in the icy Baltic Sea.

Febber said to Glendaloca, "You know, we've come all this way to do this; certainly a little BO is nothing compared to the experience of swimming in the frozen Baltic. I can put up with that!" And he told the attendant, "Ok, I'll take that last suit."

They put on their survival suits and jumped into the freezing water amidst the floating blocks of ice, along with the others. After bobbing around for about fifteen minutes, the crew fished them out of the water. When Febber took off his survival suit, everyone around him backed away—he positively stunk! Even the crew avoided him. Glendaloca held her nose and tried not to, but three or four feet away was as close as she could come. There was no way Febber could take a shower on the Sampo to relieve the odor.

When the Sampo returned to the base where they had started the voyage, they had to take the snowmobile safari back to Kemi. Out in the open, on the snowmobiles, the odor wasn't noticeable for the rest of the group, but it hung in the air all around Febber. Back in Kemi, they boarded the M/S Latvia for the trip back to Helsinki. The first thing Febber did was to take a shower in the small head in their small cabin as the ship got underway for the trip back. However, when Febber came out of the shower, he still stunk, maybe not *quite* as bad, but he still stunk.

Glendaloca looked at him, smelled him and said, "Febber, it's permeated into the pores of your skin. The only way you're going to get rid of that awful odor is to sit in the sauna at home for a few hours, and sweat it out."

Febber reluctantly acknowledged she was probably right. In the meantime, all the other passengers on the M/S Latvia stayed as far away from Febber as they could.

The M/S Latvia was constructed with a double hull as had been the German-based cruise ship M/S World Discoverer, which made voyages to the Antarctic polar region. But even a double hull was not immune to danger—that ship struck an uncharted rock and listed and grounded in the Solomon Islands. On its return from Kemi the captain of the M/S Latvia wasn't concerned about rocks, but he was concerned about the huge ice floes in the North Baltic Sea. Hitting an ice floe the wrong way could put a hole even in the double hull of the ship. So the captain and his first mate were both on high alert for danger. In addition to the problem of ice floes, a storm with thirty-five to forty-five mph winds out of the west had come up, creating ten to thirteen foot high waves—not uncommon weather for the Baltic Sea.

About 9:00 p.m. that evening when they had passed Oulu on the Finnish coast and were midway between Umea on the Swedish coast and Vaasa further south on the Finnish coast, Febber got violently seasick. Most of the passengers were in the main cabin area, trying to avoid Febber anyway because he smelled so bad. When Febber ran to the starboard side of the ship to open a porthole to vomit through it, all of the other passengers ran to the port side of the ship. This may have contributed to what happened next, or it may have happened anyway, because of the wind and waves, but the ship began to heel dangerously over on the port side. Just at that moment, a large ice floe slammed into the side of the ship and then hit the propeller and the rudder which were lifted up by the ship rolling over so far on the port side. The propeller bent and the pins holding the rudder broke, causing the ship to completely lose both steerage and steerageway. The ship was now at the mercy of the wind and the waves. The captain frantically put out "Mayday" distress calls on the ship's radio.

Captain Gustave Neiderbaum and his crew on the Beneficial Ringer had just stowed the last of the boxes of herring packed in ice in the ship's hold. They were as far north as they had ever trawled, and were ready to head back south to Helsinki. Gustave heard the Mayday calls on his radio and realized that the distressed M/S Latvia was only several kilometers north of them. He put the Beneficial Ringer into full speed ahead on a course directly to the troubled ship. When they got close, they could see that the M/S Latvia was listing badly to the port side, as well as not being able to maneuver in the high seas. Each succeeding huge wave was causing it to list more and more to the port side. It was obvious that the vessel might capsize at any time.

Gustave brought the Beneficial Ringer around to the starboard side of the M/S Latvia to attempt to transfer some of the passengers, but it was too dangerous. The ships banged together twice, and Gustave feared if they banged together one more time, the hull of his ship would rupture. At the next trough between the waves, he gunned the engine to bring the Beneficial Ringer ahead of the M/S Latvia. At the same time Eustis threw a line attached to a mooring hawser to the troubled ship. A crew member caught it and three of the crew, aided by a number of passengers, pulled in the line and then the hawser, and secured it to a cleat on the deck of the M/S Latvia.

Gustave tried to keep the boats close, his in front of the other, so passengers could transfer to his ship. But that also caused the bow of the M/S Latvia to occasionally crash onto the stern of his ship. In spite of the pitching and rolling of the two ships, passengers did move from the M/S Latvia to the Beneficial Ringer. They did this by jumping from the bow of the M/S Latvia when it was close to and almost above the stern of the trawler. Many were injured when they hit the deck. Skaggs and Gus helped by grabbing passengers as soon as they were on the deck which was still slippery with ice and fish scales, so they would not slide off and go over the low gunwales into the sea. The dogs also pushed them toward the hatch to the hold. The hold was the safest place to be, in order to avoid being swept overboard by a wave. While this was going on, Eustis was throwing boxes of fish overboard as fast as he could, to lighten the boat and to make room for more and more passengers in the hold.

More people were jumping than the two dogs could catch at the same time, and one did go over the side—it was Febber! Gus jumped in after him; Skaggs ran to get Gustave, as he had done two years earlier when Gus had rescued Eustis, and Gustave rushed from the fo'c'sle to pull Febber to safety as Gus brought him close to the side of the ship. As Gustave was leaning over the gunwale pulling in Febber, the two boats crashed together again. The bow of the Latvia crashed down on the stern gunwale of the trawler crushing Gustave's left leg. He still hung on to Febber, and with the help of one of the uninjured passengers pulled him out of the icy water. If they hadn't acted so fast, Febber would have frozen to death. The passenger then pulled Gus on board. Then he and another quickly got Gustave on the deck and applied a tourniquet to stop the blood flowing from his leg.

Unbelievably, all of the passengers and crew got off of the M/S Latvia and onto the much smaller trawler. Eustis then cut the hawser holding the two vessels together, just as the next wave—a huge one—crashed into both boats. The Latvia heeled even further to port, and then the bow of the ship slowly nosed over into the water. For a minute or so, the ship was vertical in the water, slowly bobbing up and down with the stern in the air, and sinking ever so slowly. Then there was a loud "whoosh" sound and the M/S Latvia disappeared from sight as it slipped below the surface of the water and sank to the bottom of the Baltic Sea.

The M/S Latvia thus joined a much larger sister ship, the M/S Estonia which sunk in the Baltic Sea in September, 1994, on its way to Stockholm. Heavy gales had made steerage and maintaining speed difficult for that ship also. Some believed that open doorways at the prow of the ship allowed water to seep into the main deck, causing the ship to heel onto her starboard side. Eight hundred fifty-two lives were lost when that ship sank. In the case of the M/S Latvia, a much smaller vessel, the combination of water seeping through a small gash in the hull caused by the ice floe, together with all of the passengers rushing to the port side to avoid Febber, probably initiated the heeling of the ship and its sinking. Thanks to the quick action by Gustave Neiderbaum and his crew no lives were lost when the M/S Latvia sank.

The worst injury on the Beneficial Ringer was to Gustave Neiderbaum. A crew member from the M/S Latvia and a passenger who was a doctor attended to him. The captain of the M/S Latvia, Captain Erik Johan Anders, took over control of the trawler and headed for the nearest port, which was Vaasa. All of the rescued passengers had to stay packed together in the hold of the ship. It was like the Tokyo subway at rush hour—everyone was crushed together. But that was the safest place to be. The deck was slippery and dangerous, and huge waves kept crashing over the gunwales. Having all of the passengers in the hold also provided ballast. Captain Anders expertly navigated the troughs and heights of the waves, and kept the ship on its southeasterly course to Vaasa. It was only forty-five minutes before the lights of the buildings in Vaasa came into view. Captain Anders brought the ship in behind the breakwater and then to the dock in the harbor. An ambulance was waiting on the quay. As soon as the boat docked and he could be carried off, it quickly sped off with Gustave Neiderbaum inside on a stretcher, its siren blaring.

When he arrived at the hospital, Gustave was delirious and in shock. His left leg had to be amputated. He woke up the next morning and learned that he no longer had his leg. He began to remember what had happened the day before. They had a hold full of fish, and were ready to return to Helsinki. Then the Mayday signal had come. He had maneuvered his boat to try to rescue the people on the distressed ship. He remembered Eustis throwing the boxes of fish into the sea, and Skaggs and Gus keeping the passengers who were jumping onto his boat from sliding into the sea. He remembered Gus going after Febber who went overboard, and then trying to pull Febber from the icy water. He remembered the searing pain in his leg—actually in his whole body—and didn't remember anything after that. He thought he must have passed out.

Gustave began to think about what would happen next. He realized that the loss of the catch of fish would mean he would not be able to make the next payment on the mortgage he had on the Beneficial Ringer. And without a leg, he would not be able to fish again, maybe never, or at least for a very long time. The Handelsbanken would foreclose its mortgage on the Beneficial Ringer, for sure.

Febber and Glendaloca came to the hospital with Eustis, Skaggs and Gus. The two dogs had to wait outside; they were not allowed in the hospital. Febber thanked Gustave for saving his life and he and Glendaloca said they would do anything they could to help him. They told him what had happened after his leg was crushed, and how Captain Anders had brought the Beneficial Ringer to Vaasa. They told him Captain Anders was arranging for an ambulance to take Gustave to Helsinki. With Gustave's permission, he would take the trawler to Helsinki. Eustis said he would ride back on the trawler and take Skaggs and Gus with him.

Back in Helsinki, Gustave had several operations to close and tie the remaining tendons, ligaments, and blood vessels in the stump of his leg, and to close its end. After some time, he would begin rehabilitation, and later still he was told he could get a prosthesis. He had a lot of time to think. He knew he could not take care of Skaggs and Gus; Gus particularly needed a lot of exercise. Skaggs was now an old dog, and was starting to walk slowly most of the time. Eustis had been a big help, but he was looking for another job. Gustave thought he would be fine; Eustis had grown immensely as a person while working as a deckhand on the Beneficial Ringer. His attitude was always positive and he focused with all his energy on whatever task he was given, and did not quit until he had finished it. And because of that he did whatever he had to do right, the first time, every time. Now he would be a success at whatever he did.

Even though Gustave was in no condition to take care of the dogs, there was no way he could part with Skaggs. Skaggs had been with him ever since his stop in Labrador, and was like his right hand. Skaggs had done all manner of things for Gustave, and was his best friend and companion to boot. And Skaggs was old; he did not have much time left. Gustave would keep Skaggs for as long as he lived, and Skaggs could fetch things for him and help him recover from his injury. He felt almost the same way about Gus; Gus was as smart, loyal, hardworking, and good a dog as a man could have. But for a while at least, he knew it would be very difficult for him to keep both dogs. Lots of people would love to have Gus, he was sure. But he could not bear to part with him, either.

And then he remembered his Aunt Ethelene and Uncle Evanar and his visit to see them in West Jefferson, Ohio, in the United States. They had been so impressed with Skaggs they practically begged him to consider them if he ever had a dog like that that needed a home. The thought occurred to him: he could send Gus to live with Ethelene and Evanar. And maybe, just maybe, there was the possibility, if he could come up with the money, sometime later he might be able to go to the United States to have his prosthesis fitted, and see Gus again. He could ask Febber and Glendaloca to make the arrangements for Gus.

Later, as he lay in his hospital bed, he began to feel sorry for himself. Although the pain was beginning to lessen in the stump of his leg, the uncertainty of his future was now taking a greater toll on his spirit. It was hard for him to imagine what he might do next. He felt worse than he had ever felt since the accident.

Suddenly he heard a knock, and the door to his room opened. He turned his head and saw Safiina standing in the doorway. At that moment, sunlight from the small window in the room bathed directly on her. With her blonde hair, she looked absolutely radiant.

For almost a minute, neither spoke. They had not seen each other since the "party" at the Hilton Helsinki Kalastajatorppa hotel more than three years before.

Safiina spoke first. "Gustave, I heard about what happened in the Baltic, and all the people you saved, and the accident on your boat. I'm so sorry, but I'm also so proud of you!" She moved to the side of his bed and looked down at him. Her eyes moistened, and then she bent over to give him a kiss.

She paused with her head six inches from his. Their eyes met and the look between them seemed to penetrate their souls. At that moment, each realized they would be forever joined.

Two weeks later, Gus found himself inside a small fiberglass crate, being loaded into the cargo bay of a Boeing airliner. He was being loaded onto US Airways flight 782, outbound from Helsinki to Cleveland, Ohio, but Gus didn't know that. He knew he was in a very small crate, and could hardly turn around, and he didn't know what was happening. He missed Gustave and Skaggs. The crate jostled as the conveyor belt took it up into the plane, and then again as all sorts of baggage was crammed around it. When the crate had been outside, he could at least see sunlight coming in through the small window on each side near the top of the crate. Now everything was dark. He heard the cargo bay door slam shut, and then a loud "click" as the latch securing it was closed. Then all was quiet. But not for long. Fifteen minutes later the engines started, and the sound they made increased in intensity and pitch as the captain applied more power. Soon the plane was moving, and then faster, and faster, and the sounds and sensations Gus heard and felt were like nothing he had ever experienced.

Gus was a sea dog, strong, rough, and tough. But Gus was not just strong physically; he was also strong mentally. He had no sense of fear, or anxiety, or helplessness. He always embodied supreme confidence; that was just the way he was. He didn't worry about where he was, or what was happening. He simply lay in his crate and settled in for a long nap.

As he lay in his crate in the cargo bay of Flight 782, under and surrounded by luggage, there is no way Gus could have known that four years earlier his father had been on that very same flight, from Helsinki to Cleveland, Ohio. Or that his father had made the flight sleeping in a first class seat, far above where he now was in the plane.

CHAPTER 8

ANN!! GET ME A BUD!

One summer afternoon four years before Gus found himself amidst the baggage in the cargo hold of a flight from Helsinki to Cleveland, Ohio, Jimmey Jae Jammison had just finished a week long over-the-road trip driving his eighteen-wheeler semi-trailer tractor truck from Roundville, Ohio, to Phoenix, Arizona, and back. He was an "owner-operator," meaning that he owned his tractor and worked as an independent contractor. He picked up trailers and hauled freight for a variety of trucking companies. This trip had been for the FastExpress Trucking Company. He parked the trailer at their distribution center two miles east of Roundville, and headed home.

Jimmey Jae was tired, stiff and sore from driving and living in the rig for a week. He looked forward to getting home and seeing his wife and daughter. Using his side mirrors, he backed the tractor into the driveway of his modest home on the outskirts of Roundville. As the house came in view in the mirror, he saw his wife at the front bay window of the house waiting for him. Then Kandy Kae Jammison disappeared from the window as she ran to the door and fairly flew down the steps to greet her husband. Jimmey Jae jumped down from the tractor and embraced her with a passionate kiss that swept her off of her feet. As it always did, the kiss left her tingling and breathless and limp. Jimmey Jae may not have always been the best husband, and he did have a number of faults that Kandy Kae put up with, and he was gone a lot, but all the doubts she often felt about her man were erased by the kiss Jimmey Jae gave her when he returned from his trips. Jimmey Jae was the consummate kisser!

Their daughter, however, did not run out the front door as her mother had. Jennie Mae Jammison, age 15, was at that awkward age when parents were boorish noobs. It was definitely uncool to run out the door and throw your arms around your father. Jennie Mae wouldn't chance being seen doing such a thing. She stayed in her room with the door shut and pretended to be absorbed with her computer.

Jennie Mae was not one of the popular girls in school. She was on the chubby side and wore glasses. This accentuated her natural shyness. The consequence was that she was often the butt of jokes or teasing, which the perpetrators regarded as harmless fun, but to Jennie Mae stung. It never occurred to the girls who teased her that it was mean. However, Kandy Kae had often seen her daughter come home in tears and go to her room where she would disappear behind the locked door until dinnertime. Kandy Kae tried to talk about this problem with Jimmey Jae, but they never had any realistic discussion.

Jimmey Jae's typical response was, "Tell me who those damn kids are who're tormenting Jennie Mae and I'll blow their heads off!!" If not that, he would spout something like, "I'll tan their butts!!" Jimmey Jae and Kandy Kae were both graduates of Roundville High, but they had no training or clue as to how to confront or deal with this problem, or how to negotiate with people, for that matter.

That weekend they had a backyard barbeque with one of Jimmey Jae's hunting buddies and his wife. The men liked to get together and tell stories about their hunting experiences. Jimmey Jae owned several of the most popular hunting rifles. He had a Winchester Model 70, with a detachable box magazine, a Browning A-Bolt, and a Remington Model 700. He also had a Ruger American Rifle (a semi-automatic), and a Colt .45 automatic pistol, which he carried in his truck. When it was not hunting season, his favorite pastime was to go to the shooting range and blast away at shooting targets. These targets were not just round circles with a bulls-eye in the center. Some were small animals on a spring, which would flip over when hit. Others would spin around, some would hop and roll around on the ground, and some of the targets would even explode! That made it even more fun, but since these explosive targets were the most expensive (and not reusable) they were always saved for the last round.

Adolphus and Rhonda Rae Roudabusher arrived for the barbeque party.

"Hey, Jimmey Jae, did ya shoot eny a them coyotees down ther in Arizone? Adolphus yelled to Jimmey, when he first saw him. Adolphus was Jimmey's best friend and shooting buddy.

Jimmey shot back, "No you dumb-ass! This was business! I didn't have time to go shoot any damn coyotees. I had to deliver a bunch of framing steel and bring back a load of mesquite for the charcoal factory. You 'n' I'll go out tomorrow and shoot 'em up!" By this he meant they would go to the range for target practice.

"Here, have a Bud!" he told his friend, offering him a beer.

Kandy Kae and Rhonda Rae moved to the other side of the table where they could talk about Rhonda Rae's latest experiences as a Mary Kay cosmetics sales lady. Rhonda Rae was as enthusiastic about selling cosmetics as Jimmey Jae and Adolphus were about guns. Rhonda Rae's ambition was to make enough money from her business to someday have a pink Cadillac, like the original Mary Kay.

While Jimmey Jae and Adolphus were carrying on with their hunting or target shooting stories, Kandy Kae and Rhonda Rae were going over all the gossip that invariably accompanied selling Mary Kay cosmetics. This time the conversation revolved around a "client" (who shall remain nameless) who was trying to spruce herself up to be attractive to her husband, who had not shown much interest in her recently, which led to speculation about whether he was having an affair, and since everyone in Roundville knew practically everyone else, who the paramour might be (if he was having an affair!). That discussion could easily consume an hour or more.

The cosmetics business involves selling hope and image as much or more than products. It's hard work, and frequently difficult. Rhonda Rae remarked that the "client" they had been talking about had bristles on her upper lip that made her look like a porcupine.

Kandy Kae asked, "What did you sell her?"

"Lipstick," replied Rhonda Rae. "She tried ruby red, pink, and then red mahogany."

"Did it make her look any better?"

"Nope." said Rhonda Rae. "You can put lipstick on a porcupine, but it's still a porcupine."

"Yeah, I guess so," said Kandy Kae.

"You know what they say," said Ronda Rae, "if you got a pig, you can dress it up, but it's still a pig."

Then, after making that aphorism, Rhonda Rae asked—in a particularly inappropriate juxtaposition of subject matters—about Jennie Mae. "Are the kids at school still being mean to Jennie Mae?"

When he heard this, Jimmey Jae's ears perked up and the men stopped their conversation to listen.

"It hasn't stopped," said Kandy Kae. "She's teased mercilessly. I wish she had something to make her feel special, and good about herself."

Rhonda Rae thought out loud, "Maybe she could be a contestant for the Miss Pumpkin crown." The Roundville Pumpkin Show was a month away, and applications to be a contestant in this local pageant were being submitted to the selection committee that week.

"No," Kandy Kae replied, "She's probably too young, and anyway, if she were rejected as a contestant, that would be even worse."

Adolphus then piped up, "Why don't you get her a dog?! A dog would be a good companion and make her feel good. A lot of kids don't have their own dog. So she would be something special."

A thought hit Jimmey Jae. "I could get her a huntin' dog. She could take care of it during the week when I'm gone, and it could go huntin' with me on the weekends in huntin' season. That's a great idea!"

Kandy Kae wasn't so sure about this idea. It seemed like Jimmey Jae just wanted a hunting dog—which so far he couldn't have, because he was gone so much—and wanted Jennie Mae to take care of it.

"It has to be her dog, not yours," she said.

"OK, OK, it will be her dog. But it can also hunt with me," he said. "And the NRA has a program to teach kids to use guns. Maybe she can do that and then go with me and the dog huntin' too."

So that's how it came about that Jennie Mae got a dog. Adolphus told them about a champion field dog that had just had a litter of puppies, and he and Jimmey Jae went the next day and got the pick of the litter. It was a female American Labrador retriever, chocolate color. It came from a long line of champion field dogs. These Labradors had been bred to do field work, and over the years the strain had evolved to be taller, thinner and faster than their English cousins. They also had a longer muzzle, a thinner head and tail, and were not as muscular. Kandy Kae insisted that it would be Jennie Mae's dog, even though she didn't get to pick it out. Jimmey Jae agreed, figuring he could go hunting with the dog when he wanted to, even though it was his daughter's dog.

Jennie Mae loved the new puppy. She named her Ann. She liked the name Ann because it was different from other names in Roundville, most of which were really two names. But her dad had the papers to register Ann as a purebred Labrador retriever. He couldn't change the dog's first name, as he had told his daughter it was her dog, but he did add a last name. When he filled out the application he gave the dog two names. Jennie Mae didn't know it, but Ann's full name on her American Kennel Club registration was Ann Heuser, named for the brewery that made her dad's favorite beer.

When Jennie Mae first got Ann Heuser, she was only eight weeks old. Ann was only a small puppy, but she exuded confidence and energy. She somehow got into just about everything. She climbed into one of the drawers of the old chest in Jennie Mae's room that had been left open, and pulled out all of her underwear and bras and carried them around the house. She got into Kandy Kae's knitting basket and tangled up all the yarn. Then she got into the Mary Kay cosmetics Kandy Kae had purchased from Rhonda Rae Roudabusher, and tipped them over. The nail polish remover seeped into the face cream. The eyebrow pencil got red lipstick on it. And the shampoo spilled into the makeup pads Kandy Kae used to put makeup on her face.

But the next mess actually changed everything. It was the mess that changed Ann's destructive behavior to constructive behavior. It happened this way: the following Monday night, Jimmey Jae had left his can of Budweiser on the table beside his Naugahyde Barcalounger in front of his big screen TV, where he was watching WWE Raw professional wrestling, when he went to the kitchen to make himself a bologna sandwich (he called it a baloney sandwich). Ann saw it and took his beer off the table. She spilled it all over the floor when she ran from the living room to the kitchen carrying it sideways in her mouth. She liked Jimmey Jae and thought she was being a good dog by bringing his beer to him. Jimmey Jae didn't initially understand and was about to start yelling bad words at Ann and give her a swat, when a light bulb went off. The dog was trying to bring him his beer! All he had to do was show her how to hold the can of beer properly (if it was open) and she could run and get it for him. She could do all kinds of errands!

So that is how Ann first learned to get beers for people. Jimmey Jae wanted Budweiser, so she got him the red can out of the fridge (which she quickly learned to open with her paw). She got the blue can (Bud Light) for Adolphus Roudabusher, when he came to visit, because he liked Bud Light. And she would get a can of Orange Crush—the orange can—for Kandy Kae, and the green can—a Seven-up—for Jennie Mae. After Ann learned these simple chores, Jennie Mae found it was easy to teach her to do other useful things, and all sorts of tricks. Jennie Mae had Ann show off for some of her friends, and then more and more of the girls at school wanted to see Jennie Mae and her dog. She let the ones who were nice to her pet and play with Ann.

As the year went on, Ann Heuser grew bigger and bigger, until she was fully grown at eleven months, and weighed 72 pounds. Jennie Mae began to take on the enthusiasm, confidence and energy of her dog. She started running with Ann for a mile and a half at a time, and then two miles, and finally three miles. The exercise of working and running with Ann caused her lose weight. Her young body became toned, and her appearance became radiant. She got contacts, and ditched her glasses. Jennie Mae's spirit and personality began to glow. She slowly became one of the girls the others wanted to be around. The group that was the "in" group wasn't so "in" anymore, and one-by-one they gravitated to the new group that was forming with Jennie Mae in the center.

At the same time Ann Heuser was learning to bring beers and do other errands and tricks, Jimmey Jae was teaching her to be a great field dog. She learned to move on whistle commands and on hand signal commands, either straight ahead, or to the right, or to the left in the field. She learned to fetch rabbits, quail, grouse, and pheasant on command. And she learned to swim after and retrieve ducks and geese from Lake Chargoggagoggmanchaugger. The name of the lake, which is two miles south of Roundville, translates roughly to "You fish on your side, I fish on my side, and nobody fish in the middle."

Boys began to notice Jennie Mae. She discouraged some, and encouraged others, and finally made her choice. She and Zachary Whackendack really hit it off. He became her "steady" boyfriend. Zach was a smart kid who not only got good grades without having to study very much; he had lots of interests and continually came up with fun things to do. One of his ideas was to enter Jennie Mae in the Miss Pumpkin contest in the annual pumpkin shows which are held in October.

Zach sent Jennie Mae's pictures and application to be a Miss Pumpkin contestant to the Circleville Pumpkin Show, the largest pumpkin festival in the state. But they rejected her. So Zachary sent fourteen pictures of her to the Roundville Pumpkin Show committee charged with selecting the candidates for their Miss Pumpkin. He followed up his submission of the pictures by calling each member of the committee and lobbying for her. His efforts were rewarded and she was chosen to be a contestant. This was really a big deal. Being accepted by the rival show was sweet, and made Jennie Mae absolutely determined to win.

The Roundville Pumpkin show was not as old or as large as the Circleville Pumpkin Show, which dated from 1903. Roundville's show started in 1986. But it ran for four full days, and each year seemed to get bigger and bigger, with more events. The selection of Miss Pumpkin was on the second day of the show, and the winner would preside over the subsequent events. Because she had been rejected by Circleville, Jennie Mae felt a lot of pressure, not just to win the contest. Since comparisons were always made between the Miss Pumpkin winners in the two towns, she felt she was really competing in two events.

On October 16 Jennie Mae Jammison was primping in front of the mirror in her bedroom. She was getting ready for the final judging in the Miss Pumpkin pageant later that evening. Adding to the pressure of competing in this pumpkin pageant was the fact that her dog, Ann, had a litter of puppies seven weeks before. Jennie Mae was worried about finding homes for the pups. The mother dog, Ann Heuser, was taking good care of them, but it would soon be time for them to have their own homes and owners.

Zach arrived at her house to at 8:00 p.m. to take her to the Lincoln Street Stage where the judging of the Miss Pumpkin contestants would start at 9:00 p.m. Before leaving, Jennie Mae insisted on showing Zach the puppies again. (He had already seen them about a dozen times). There were ten of them, all chocolate, four males and six females.

Jennie Mae remarked, "I really hope we can find good homes for all of them; it seems like everyone in this town already has a dog." She thought a moment, and then added, "And people always want a male; the females are harder to place. Nobody's answered the ad I placed yet."

Zach replied, "They're all purebreds; certainly there are people out there who'll want 'em."

Jennie Mae had a look of doubt on her face; she wasn't so sure. She wanted each puppy to go to a good home.

"Maybe I'll see someone at the show who wants a good puppy," she replied.

They turned away and went out to Zach's car to drive into town.

The judging at the Lincoln Street Stage took over two hours. It took so long because there were twelve contestants, and they had to appear in three different outfits. The first category was "Pumpkin Mania," which meant that each contestant had to dress in the most outrageous costume with a pumpkin theme. Jennie Mae dressed as a piece of pumpkin pie, in a wedge shaped costume with the crust at the top. It was complete with whipped cream. Her feet at the bottom of the wedge were so close together she could hardly walk across the stage. Her bobbling along as she walked only made the piece of pie look better, as the top wavered back and forth while the tip of the piece of pie (where her feet were) just shuffled along.

One of the judges remarked—and the remark carried all through the crowd as he did not realize his mike was turned on: "That piece of pie looks good enough to eat!"

The second category of dress for the contestants was "Pumpkins I Have Eaten." There were a lot of possibilities here. Pumpkin can be used for all kinds of food and dishes. One girl went as a pumpkin donut. Another went as a pumpkin waffle, complete with syrup. There was even a pumpkin burger. Jennie Mae went as a pumpkin cream puff.

That caused the same judge to remark, and again be heard throughout the audience, "That cream puff looks good enough to eat!"

The third and last category of dress, which was unique to the Roundville Pumpkin Show—the Circleville Pumpkin Show did not have this category—was the "Pumpkin Swim Suit" category. This was a chance for the contestants to really show off, if they wanted to. Most of them wore one-piece swim suits made of orange and black spandex. Some had suits with pumpkin images embossed on their suit. One had two small pumpkins on her chest, one on her front below the waist, and two on her behind. That got a lot of comments. But Jennie Mae stole the show. She came out in a suit of pumpkin seeds. Jennie Mae was a bosomy young girl. The pumpkin seeds were appropriately stuck to her body with body glue. And each seed was luminescent. The pumpkin seed get-up was actually not as revealing as the spandex suits worn by most of the other contestants, but the effect was spectacular. Under the spotlights that bathed the contestants with bright light she was dazzling! And when Jennie Mae left the runway and went to the side of the stage, no one even looked at the next contestant to walk down the runway. Her luminescent pumpkin seed suit fairly glowed in the darker area away from the spotlights. The men in the audience all craned their necks to get a better look at Jennie Mae. The women—most of them—covered their eyes. Then the ones with children immediately uncovered them—and covered their children's eyes.

The same judge, who had made remarks before about Jennie Mae's other costumes, started to say, "That pumpkin girl looks …"

And at that point he was slapped across the face by one of the female judges who hissed at him, *"Don't say it!"*

One of the other contestants claimed that Jennie Mae should be disqualified, because she had used a food motif for all three categories, when in fact they were distinct categories. But this objection was overruled. The five male judges all voted for Jennie Mae as Miss Pumpkin, and they carried the day over the objections of the four female judges. Jennie Mae was crowned Miss Pumpkin and given a four-foot-tall trophy, which consisted of a bronze pumpkin with a female figurine rising out of it, with a crown on her head.

The Pumpkin show involved a lot more than just the contest Jennie Mae had won. There was a pumpkin carving contest, bands and entertainers, tap dancers, a fashion show, a pumpkin pie eating contest, square dancing, a dog show, an egg tossing contest, a hula hoop contest, and numerous parades to mention just a few of the events. There was a whole area set aside for amusement rides, including a Ferris wheel, a merry-go-round, go-cart races, fun houses, and many more. Throughout the whole show area were lots of booths selling all manner of things to eat, from sausage sandwiches to pumpkin pies. This year two new events had been added, which the organizers hoped would really set the Roundville Pumpkin Show apart and cause it to pull ahead of the Circleville Pumpkin show in attendance and prestige. These were a pumpkin shooting contest, sponsored by the National Rifle Association, and a gigantic pumpkin fireworks display on the last night of the show.

Jimmy Jae Jammison was one of the organizers of the pumpkin shooting contest, but it was really Jennie Mae's boyfriend, Zach Whackendack, who came up with the idea that made it so impressive. That was to use the Ferris wheel to hurl pumpkins high into the air, as targets for contestants to shoot at. Arms were rigged to each spoke of the Ferris wheel, with a large cup-like container at the end of each arm. Three pumpkins were placed in each cup, and a release mechanism held the pumpkins in place. The contestants all gathered at a spot about a hundred yards south of the Ferris wheel. While they were gathering, the last of the riders on the Ferris wheel were told to disembark, and no more were loaded. At 2:00 p.m. the contest began.

Ekze Keese, the Ferris wheel operator, started it up, and then slowly doubled the normal speed of the wheel, so it was really rotating at a high rate of speed. As a spoke of the wheel with the extended arm holding three pumpkins approached an angle about 80 degrees from the ground, the release mechanism was triggered and the three pumpkins flew from the arm high into the air. Only three pumpkins were released on each rotation of the Ferris wheel, so the air would not be full of pumpkins. This was a big Ferris wheel: it had been brought in from Chicago, and was 150 feet tall and had 40 spokes, loaded with 120 pumpkins. This meant that it had to stop and be reloaded after 40 revolutions of throwing pumpkins.

Taking into account the circumference, radius, and speed of the Ferris wheel, and the fact that the pumpkins weighed between 8 and 12 pounds each, Zachary Whackendack had computed a range of trajectories to determine the size and location of the area where the pumpkins would fall if they were not hit. That area was then cordoned off so no one would be hit by a flying pumpkin. A huge crowd gathered to watch the pumpkin shooting contest. Jennie Mae was there with Ann, and her job was to help keep the crowd away from the restricted area. Jennie Mae was an attraction in herself, in a white flowing dress and her Miss Pumpkin Crown on her blond head. Ann stayed at her side and occasionally got between Jennie Mae and any spectator who tried to get too close to her.

The contest created an extreme adrenaline rush for the shooters. They shot in rotation at each launch of three flying pumpkins. A shooter could get one, two, or three points, if he hit one or more of the pumpkins, or no points if he missed all of them. Then the next shooter would take his turn to hit the next three flying pumpkins. Jimmey Jae and Adolphus were never more excited. Jimmey Jae yelled to his friend, "This's better than shooting at them exploding targets!!" Of the 25 shooters in the contest, they were leading in points. The contest went for five rounds apiece, which meant that 375 medium size pumpkins were hurled into the air to be shot at. 298 were hit, so bits of pumpkin were falling out of the sky over the whole area. But 77 were not hit, which meant that 77 medium size pumpkins weighing between 8 and 12 pounds each crashed to the ground and splattered all over the place. Fortunately, Zach's calculations were right on; they all landed in the restricted area.

However, with all the pumpkins flying into the air, the sound of the gunshots, and the crash of an occasional pumpkin hitting the ground—to say nothing of the flying bits of pumpkins that were hit—three of the younger children in the crowd got so excited they began running around collecting pieces of fallen pumpkin. Their frenzy to pick up pieces of pumpkin was contagious, and in a few moments a whole crowd of kids was running out to where the pumpkin bits were falling, to join in the game. This was actually quite dangerous; occasionally whole pumpkins were still falling to the ground. It wasn't possible to immediately stop the Ferris wheel to prevent more pumpkins from being launched, and they kept flying.

Jennie Mae yelled to Ann, *"Go bring the kids back here!"* Ann took off at full speed, ran to the first child, grabbed his sleeve and pulled him back out of the cordoned off area. Then she ran to the next child and did the same, and then the next, and the next. At the same time, Jimmey Jae realized that a bunch of children were now in the cordoned off area and in danger of being hit by falling pumpkins.

He yelled to all of the other shooters, *"Everybody shoot!!"*

With everyone shooting at the pumpkins being launched, there was much less chance that one would be missed and fall to earth and hit one of the children. In a few more moments, Ann had all of the children out of the danger area. Zachary Whackendack, who was trying to oversee the contest, called a break in the action and had Ekze Keese, the operator, stop the Ferris wheel. The children were cautioned not to leave the safe area again. Then they reloaded the Ferris wheel with pumpkins, and resumed the contest.

When the pumpkin shooting finished, Jimmey Jae was the winner with the most points. Adolphus was second. Ann was praised for so quickly rounding up the children who had gone out of the safe area and everyone gave her a big round of applause. Jimmey Jae thought it was especially sweet when his daughter, Jennie Mae, presented him with the first prize trophy, a bronze pumpkin with a rifle thrust through it and protruding on each side. He beamed and was fairly bursting with pride that both he and his daughter had taken first place in the events they had entered.

The gigantic pumpkin fireworks display was to begin that evening, and would be the last event of the pumpkin festival. It was highly advertised, and people from all over the county and nearby counties were expected to come to watch the show. Because the pumpkin shooting contest had been such a success, the plan was to again use the Ferris wheel to hurl pumpkins into the air. This time they would be packed with fireworks. Zachary Whackendack, who was probably the most level-headed of the group that was planning the event, realized that staging it at night with such a huge crowd presented more of a risk than had the pumpkin shooting contest. Since the weight of the pumpkins would be a little heavier (each one being packed with fireworks), Ekze Keese was told to increase the speed of the Ferris wheel one notch faster than had been used for the pumpkin shoot, so they would be launched high enough into the air. Zach took this into account when he computed a new landing area. Even though all the pumpkins were expected to explode in the air, Zach still went over his calculations three times to compute their trajectory. It was always possible that one might not explode and fall to the ground.

That evening, at 9:00 p.m. when it was dark, the pumpkin fireworks show began. Three hundred sixty new pumpkins (120 for each full round in the Ferris wheel), each packed with a variety of fireworks, were on hand. These pumpkins had also been painted with the same luminescent paint that Zach and Jennie Mae had used to paint the pumpkin seeds for her swim suit. The first 120 were loaded into the 40 launchers on the ends of the 40 spokes of the wheel. Ekze was told to start the Ferris wheel, and bring it up to speed. This time Zach had included an ignition device in each launcher which ignited a fuse to each pumpkin as it was launched. When the Ferris wheel reached the predetermined velocity, the release mechanism on the launchers activated. As each pumpkin left its launcher, the fuse to the fireworks inside dragged through the igniter, lighting it. Luminescent pumpkins began flying sky high, and in moments pumpkins began exploding high in the night air. The noise of the explosions, the colored streaming of the fireworks, and the scattering bits of luminescence falling out of the sky over a wide area was incredible! It was beyond spectacular! The crowd cheered wildly, clapping their hands and jumping up and down in excitement.

The Ferris wheel operator, Ekze Keese, was a drifter who had caught on with the carnival that furnished the Ferris wheel. He was as excited as everyone else by the pumpkin fireworks, but unfortunately he decided to do something he thought would make the show even better. For the last round of pumpkins, Ekze decided to speed up the Ferris wheel even more than Zach had instructed. Suddenly pumpkins were going higher in the air, and further out away from the wheel (and the cordoned off landing area!). They were also going faster as they left the launching arms of the Ferris wheel, and the fuses were not igniting because they were pulled too fast through the igniters. Luminescent pumpkins were being flung so high into the air they disappeared from sight, and then reappeared again as they fell to earth. Pumpkins began bombarding the overflow parking lot west of the festival area, and many of them exploded as they hit the ground.

About this time, a young family was headed back to their car which was in the overflow parking lot, furthest away from the festival grounds. Hunk and Sally Sames had left before the show was over because their youngest child, Isabella, had fallen asleep—even as the fireworks were exploding—as it was way past her bedtime. The three other young children, Esther, Jamie and Davie, were getting tired and cranky, and Hunk and Sally thought it best to head on back to the car and beat the traffic which would be sure to jam the roadways when the show was over. They also had with them their twelve-year-old chocolate Lab, Chocolate Molly. Molly was an old dog, and now lagged behind as she could no longer keep up. Hunk and Sally knew her time was short and that she had a hard time walking, but they could not bear to put her down. They did not want to leave her alone, which was why they had taken her with the family to watch the fireworks.

Just as they were approaching their old Dodge Caravan, one of the pumpkins hit the ground in front of them and exploded. Then another fell to their left and exploded; a moment later, another exploded behind them. It was like they were literally in a war zone! Hunk yelled to the kids, *"Run for the car!"* He popped open the right sliding door of the van, and the family scrambled as fast as they could into the safety of the large vehicle.

Hunk and Sally looked around the van: Isabella, Esther, Jamie and Davie were all accounted for and safe. But Chocolate Molly was nowhere to be seen.

"Where's Molly?" Sally screamed.

Hunk looked out the window toward where they had been, and saw a dark object on the ground fifty or so feet away. He leaped from the vehicle and ran to it. It was Molly. She did not respond to his frantic cry to her. She was still, and unmoving. Hunk lifted her head, and realized she was dead. She had not been hit by a falling or exploding pumpkin, but had died of a heart attack. The shock of the explosions had been too much for the old dog. The fright from the pumpkin war zone had done her in. Her heart couldn't take it. She had frozen with fear, and her heart had stopped beating. She had died quickly and without pain.

With tears in his eyes, Hunk carried Molly back to the van, and put her in the rear compartment. Then he told his family that Molly had died. The van was dead silent. It was like the air had gone out of a brightly colored balloon. Molly had been with them all her life, and was like another child in the family.

Slowly, Hunk took a deep breath, and then he and the family drove over to the Ferris wheel. The pumpkin fireworks were now over, and people were starting to leave. Jimmey Jae, Zach and Ekze were standing next to the large Ferris wheel, watching the crowd depart. Then they were going to discuss the process of cleaning up the area and dismantling the launching arms. A large group of volunteers had gathered to help with this work. As Hunk and Sally drove up in their van, one of them approached the vehicle waving his arms, intending to tell them they could not park in that area.

Hunk stopped the van. He got out and walked up to the group, his grief over Molly's death now turning to anger.

He yelled at the crowd, "You all killed our dog with your flying pumpkins! We were bombarded with pumpkins, and you killed Molly!"

Jimmey Jay and the others gathered around, shocked by what Hunk had said.

Jimmey Jae asked, "What're you talking about? What happened, anyway?"

They had seen the pumpkins flying and not exploding in the air, but thought they flew so far away that they all came down far from the crowd of spectators.

Hunk told them all, "We went back to our car in the back lot. All of a sudden, we were bombarded with flying, exploding pumpkins. The shock of it all killed our dog."

At that, he went back to the van and opened the back and picked up an inert Molly to show everyone. Jimmey Jae, Zach, Ekze and the others gathered around. Jennie Mae came up to the group with Ann. Hunk started talking about what his family felt when the pumpkins were falling and exploding all around them.

"It was the scariest thing ever," he said. "We all hit the ground, and then we ran. The kids did great running for the car."

Sally piped in, "It was like one of those war movies, like being right in it. It was like being in *Saving Private Ryan*, or something."

She continued, "But, hey, but Molly didn't make it. Hunk went back for her, but she didn't make it." Sally started to cry. "She died because of those exploding pumpkins!"

Jimmey Jae and then the others apologized profusely. "We're really sorry," he said again and again. "You know, we're just a bunch of people here trying to put on a good show for everybody. We weren't trying to scare you or hurt your dog."

He thought for a moment and then said, "Hey, we don't have much, but maybe to try to make it up to you, we'll give you and your family lifetime passes to the Roundville Pumpkin Festival."

This really wasn't anything, because there wasn't any charge for going to the festival.

However, Jimmey Jae's overture sounded pretty good to Hunk, who said, "Gee, thanks, we would appreciate that. That's something. None of the kids got hurt, which is a good thing, and we did enjoy the pumpkin festival."

Jimmey Jae then continued, "We're sorry about your dog, too."

After a pause, he blurted out, "Well, she was an old dog, so now you don't have to put her down, so maybe that was a good thing."

Jennie Mae was shocked at this from her dad. She said, "Dad, that's an awful thing to say. These people just lost their dog because of those flying pumpkins. It doesn't matter that she was an old dog!"

Then she said, "I have an idea; maybe we could give them one of Ann's pups."

"That's a great idea; it's only fair, and I agree," said Jimmey Jae.

He turned to Hunk and Sally and told them about Ann's pups; that they were all chocolate labs, that their parents were champion field dogs, and that since their dog had died because of the pumpkin show they could have the pick of Ann's litter. Then he gave them his address and told them to come to the house with the children the next day to pick out a puppy to replace Chocolate Molly. Hunk and Sally replied that was keen of him and Jennie Mae, and that they would be there the next day.

The next morning Hunk, Sally and their four children arrived at Jimmey Jae's house. Jimmey Jae, Kandy Kae, and Jennie Mae all came out to greet them. Then they all went to the garage to see Ann's puppies. Ann's dog bed and nest where she had had the puppies was in the back. When Jimmey Jae led the group into the garage, no dogs were there. There was a doggie door in the back of the garage, so the dogs could go from inside the garage out to the back yard when the garage door was closed, and the pups had all gone outside. So the whole group went back out and around the garage to get to the back yard. There they saw Ann lying on the ground, with ten chocolate Labrador retriever puppies cavorting around, wrestling with each other, and playing with several dog balls and dog bones.

One puppy seemed to be slightly bigger than the rest. It had left the wrestling match with two of the other pups, and was exploring the yard. When Jimmey Jae and the group arrived, this puppy ran over to them and began sniffing everyone's shoes, and then jumped up on the children.

Hunk looked to Sally, who nodded in agreement. "That's the one we want," he said, pointing to the pup which was obviously the most active. "That pup has a lot of spirit! We'll pick that one."

Jimmey Jae looked at Jennie Mae. Previously, they had noticed the same pup and were thinking of keeping it for themselves. But Jimmey Jae had promised them the pick of the litter. He was in a bind. He could not go back on his word, and these people had really been nice about it, after all they had gone through with the exploding pumpkins.

So he said, "Sure, that pup is for you."

The children took turns holding the puppy, while Jimmey Jae went into the house to get the papers to give to Hunk and Sally. When he came back, he again apologized for what they had gone through the previous day, and the loss of their dog.

Hunk and Sally thanked them and said, "We'll call it even, and don't worry about it. We'll see you at the next pumpkin show!"

When they were driving to their home in West Jefferson, Ohio, Sally asked her husband, "What are we going to name this new puppy? We have to decide on a name before we send in the papers to register it."

"This dog's a female, just like Chocolate Molly" replied Hunk. "She's a replacement. Why don't we call her Chocolate Molly II, so we never forget Chocolate Molly. She was a great dog."

Both Hunk and Sally agreed: the puppy would be Chocolate Molly II.

After the Sames family drove away with the puppy, Jimmey Jae turned to the others and said, "Damn, we shouldn't have let that pup go. I can tell, it would have been the best huntin' dog we ever had. That dog had spirit; and it was the smartest pup I've ever seen at that age."

He continued, "It's all your fault, Zach, using the Ferris wheel to throw those pumpkin fireworks. If they hadn'a fallen and exploded next to those people, we never would have lost that dog! You're the cause of us losing it to them!"

Zach didn't like being blamed for the Sames family getting the dog.

He shot back, "Hey, it's not my fault. If Ekze hadn't cranked up the speed of the thing, those pumpkins all would have exploded in the air, like the first ones did, and we never would have seen those people. He caused the whole problem. It all would have worked fine if he did what I told him."

Kandy Kae who was listening to this blame game then jumped in and said, "You're both wrong. Jimmey Jae, if you hadn't promised them the pick of the litter, they never would have got the dog you wanted to keep!"

Jimmey Jae shot back, "Well, there were ten pups. They could have picked one of the nine others! I didn't cause the problem."

Jennie Mae, who was standing a bit off to the side, with Ann, couldn't stand it any longer. She had to speak up.

"You're all wrong," she said. "Sometimes stuff happens. Stuff happened."

And that's why Chocolate Molly II went to live with a family in West Jefferson, Ohio.

CHAPTER 9

MOTHER MOLLY

Hunk Sames pulled the old Dodge van into the driveway of their house on Mabeley Street in West Jefferson. The sunshine was brilliant and made the crisp air feel warmer than the car thermometer indicated. This should have been a happy occasion; coming home with a new puppy. But the brightness of the day contrasted with the emotions of the family in the car.

The Sames family was ready to be home, and ready to shake off the lingering effect Jimmey Jae had left on them. From the moment Hunk had picked Molly from the litter of Ann's pups, it had been a tense morning for everyone. Although Jimmey Jae's displeasure with Hunk's choice was unspoken, it was felt by all. Hunk and Sally felt like they couldn't get away from those people who all had two names fast enough. In addition, it was now almost 1:00 p.m., and they were all hungry. The three older children in the back seat had alternated between fidgeting and fighting the entire trip. Both Isabella, the baby, and Molly, the new pup, were crying. Sally, tired and somewhat irritated herself, didn't know which she would feed first—the baby or the new puppy.

Molly soon made the decision for her. Molly had been in the back of the van, crying because she was alone. She missed her mother and her litter mates. Isabella, the baby, was in the front of the van with Sally, crying like a typical fussy baby. When Hunk opened the right sliding door of the van, Esther, Jamie and Davie tumbled over each other to get out, and raced to the house. Sally followed with Isabella, while Hunk got Molly out of the back of the van. Sally had just set Isabella, still crying, in her baby jogger in the living room when Molly ran into her new home. Molly went right up to Isabella, and started licking her face.

Isabella was so surprised by Molly she stopped crying. She liked this brown puppy which was about as big as she was, and threw her arms around Molly's neck. Sally, not hearing any further crying, turned around to see Molly licking her baby.

"*Molly, stop that!!*" she screamed.

Molly, who liked the taste of Isabella's salty tears, kept licking even more. Sally rushed over and grabbed Isabella with one hand, and was about to swat Molly with the other, when Hunk caught her free hand and stopped her.

"Don't hit Molly," he said. "Isabella likes her!" Sally thought better of her first impulse, smiled and then quickly gave Molly a bowl of puppy chow. Then she picked up Isabella to nurse her.

From that moment, Molly and Isabella were almost inseparable. When Isabella crawled along on the floor, Molly went with her. When Isabella threw her baby rattle, Molly ran for it, picked it up and brought it back to her. Isabella would throw it again, and the two of them would play this game over and over. When it was time for Isabella to take her nap, Molly went to sleep beside her crib.

Sally soon discovered that she didn't need to stay so close to Isabella, because Molly would let her know when Isabella needed her. When Isabella would wake up and cry in her crib, Molly would find Sally and bark until Sally stopped whatever she was doing and came to take care of Isabella. If Isabella needed her diaper changed, Molly knew immediately and would run to find Sally or Hunk and bark to let them know Isabella needed help.

When Isabella got a little older, Molly actually helped her learn to walk. It happened at the coffee table. Molly saw Isabella pull herself up and then hold onto the edge of the old coffee table in the living room, trying to stand. The baby wobbled back and forth for a moment, and then lost her balance and sat down with a "thunk." Molly, who at this point was one and a half times Isabella's size, bounded over and pressed against her when she again pulled herself up by the coffee table. Isabella turned from the table and grabbed Molly's fur at the back of her neck. As Molly slowly moved away from the coffee table, Isabella, hanging on as tight as she could, kept putting one chubby leg in front of the other. She wobbled back and forth as the two of them slowly made their way across the room. Hunk and Sally were amazed. After a day or so of this, Isabella could do it by herself.

Isabella was now a toddler, the youngest child and one with a mind of her own. She didn't need any help, but Molly seemed to encourage her to get in trouble. One sunny day when both of them were outside in the backyard, Molly, who was hot, started digging a hole to lie in. Molly had found a place where the dirt was soft and black. Isabella toddled over and started to dig too, with her hands. Soon both of them were working away in a pretty good size mud hole. Isabella smeared the mud on her face, and then ate some of it. Molly, now digging with all four feet and facing away from her, was throwing mud all over her. Isabella screamed with delight; she thought it was great fun with the mud flying all around her.

Sally by chance looked out the window to see her baby, who had one muddy hand in her mouth, and her body covered with mud. She dropped the plate she was drying—she had been washing dishes—and it crashed to the floor. Sally ran for the door and practically flew into the backyard. She picked up her daughter, getting mud all over her own white dress, and ran back into the house.

"*What were you doing!*" Sally exclaimed. Isabella just smiled and gurgled. It was as if she could have talked, she knew it was better not to. Sally's ire melted. She sat Isabella in the kitchen sink, took her clothes off, and cleaned her up. Molly stayed in the mud hole in the backyard, somehow knowing this was not a good time to go back into the house.

The next day was Saturday, and Hunk planned to paint the walls in the smallest bedroom, which was Isabella's. She was the fourth child to use this room, and at this point the walls were covered with scuff marks and dirt. There was a place where someone had written on the wall with an orange crayon, which Sally had tried without complete success to remove, and another place where one of the children—they didn't know who, and no one would confess, or "rat" on who did it—had drawn a stick picture of two people and a dog on the wall with a felt tip pen. It was definitely time to paint this room, and so Isabella's crib had been moved temporarily to Hunk and Sally's room.

Hunk cleaned the walls with a mild solution of trisodium phosphate which also degreased the surface and broke the gloss of the old oil based paint which was the original paint. He finished that job, and took what was left of the cleaning solution to the garage, where he put it in a canister. Hunk knew that the solution could be toxic and planned to drop it off at a disposal facility later. Then he went back to the bedroom, opened a gallon can of light pink latex paint and began stirring it. After stirring the paint for three or four minutes, he left and went to the garage for a step ladder.

That was his big mistake. When Hunk went to get the step ladder, he left the door to the bedroom open. Molly and Isabella, who had been playing with a ball in the living room, noticed the open door. Both of them went in to the bedroom to see what Hunk had been doing. Isabella toddled up to the gallon can of pink paint, looked at it, and put her hands into it.

"Ugggg," she screamed. She reached out to wipe her hands on Molly's back. Molly didn't like the smell of the paint and jumped back. Isabella lunged toward Molly, trying to grab her with a hand wet with paint. Molly ran around the other way, causing Isabella to reverse direction, trip over her own feet and stumble into the can of paint. The paint spilled toward Molly, who ran through it, and on into the living room, leaving a trail of pink paw prints. Isabella, now crawling, slipped and fell face down in the pool of pink paint. She lay there kicking and screaming when Sally burst into the room to see what the commotion was all about.

This was a lot worse than the mud episode, and in an effort to downplay it, Hunk said, "Hey, it really would have been bad if they got into the trisodium phosphate. That could have killed or burned them!"

Sally was not pleased by the fact that Hunk could imagine something that could be worse than what had happened.

"Dammit Hunk!" she said. "I don't care about something that didn't happen. This is bad enough! Now you figure out what you are going to do about it!"

Fortunately, it was latex paint. They put Isabella in the sink again, and with soap and warm water quickly got all the paint off of her. Hunk did the same with Molly's paws, and then went to work cleaning up the bedroom and the pink paw prints that wound through the house. When he was finished cleaning up the mess he decided to forget about painting the bedroom, at least for that day.

Dogs grow a lot faster than kids, and so it wasn't very long before Molly was a lot bigger than Isabella. Isabella was fun to play with, but as Molly grew bigger she began spending more and more time with the older children, Esther, Jamie and Davie. It was fun to run with them. They went all over the neighborhood and Molly's world expanded rapidly as she started following the older kids around. Molly became well-known around West Jefferson as the Sames' kids' dog.

There was an overgrown field behind the house on Mabeley Street. There were clumps of tall weeds among a variety of tall grasses, goldenrod, ragweed, lamb's quarter and dock, mixed with thickets of scrub brush vegetation dominated by small shrubs of unknown etiology. There were lots of small hills and depressions, which made some of the scrub appear either higher or lower than it actually was. On one side of the big field was a clearing in front of a grove of saplings that reached heights of 30 or 40 feet. The children had worn paths through the dayflower, reed grass and purple mullet in this field. They had quickly learned to avoid the few patches of nettle and musk thistle.

Molly loved to follow them as they ran the paths through the weeds and grasses which in many places were taller than the children. Esther was the youngest and had a hard time keeping up, so she would often hide in one of the scrub thickets and yell for the others to find her. This would sometimes work to keep her in the game, and sometimes not—the boys might just decide to leave her there and forget about her. But Molly always came when she yelled and so Esther never felt she was alone, even when lagging behind, which was most of the time.

A year went by. One day in early summer after school was out, Jamie and Davie decided to construct a "fort" in the grove of saplings to the right of the big overgrown field. They took a saw, hammer and nails from Hunk's tool box in the garage. Esther was told to find all the long sticks she could to use in building the fort. Molly, now fully grown, saw Esther dragging a stick to the place selected for the fort, and quickly learned to do the same. With Molly helping, the two of them dragged over twenty sticks and branches they found throughout the thicket to the fort.

While Esther and Molly were dragging sticks, Jamie and Davie cut four of the smaller saplings. Then they prepared to nail the cut saplings to four of the larger trees – which were poplar trees six to seven inches in diameter, that roughly formed a square. These were the corners of the fort. The boys reached as high as they could to nail the four cut saplings horizontal against the corner trees. Then they nailed most of the other sticks lower down, horizontal on three sides of the fort. They put six sticks across the top saplings, and covered their "roof" with an old tarp they had found in the garage. Now they really had a hideout—much better than an opening in one of the scrub thickets. They could play in this fort even when it was raining, and stay dry! The three of them with Molly at their feet sat on the ground in the back of the fort and proudly contemplated their work.

It was Travis, who lived six houses down Mabeley Street, who said that the fort ought to have a cannon. Jamie and Davie had just wanted to play in the fort, and had no idea of bringing guns to the fort, let alone a cannon. Esther didn't even know what a cannon was.

Travis was a new kid who had just moved into the neighborhood. Davie met Travis one afternoon soon after they built the fort and invited him to see it. Travis was impressed.

"This is a great fort, guys," Travis remarked. "This is like the Alamo, only better. We can stand off the Mexicans here."

"What Mexicans?" asked Jamie.

Travis told him, "The Mexicans who are going to attack us and try to kick us out. We gotta get prepared! Where are the guns?! Where do you keep the ammo?"

"We don't have any guns," Davie responded. "We don't have any ammo either. We just play in this fort."

Esther, the youngest and only girl, spoke up, "I'm afraid of guns."

Travis would have none of it. He said, "What, you're all cowards. You all won't have a chance when the Mexicans attack. They'll overrun this fort and you'll all die!"

That was pretty scary. Davie had a vision of being inside the fort when it was attacked.

He asked Travis, "Will they come on horseback, like they did at the real Alamo?"

Now all the boys were thinking about the Alamo. Jamie had heard of the Battle of the Alamo at school, but didn't remember much from that. However, he and his brother, who liked John Wayne, had seen his old movie, *The Alamo*, and now they started remembering what the Alamo was all about. It wasn't very long before they too were thinking the fort would be attacked by Mexicans, and they had to get ready for a battle!

Travis continued, "There could be thousands of Mexicans! They'll have horses, and they'll have guns and bayonets! We need to get a cannon!"

That is what prompted the boys to make a cannon. Travis' uncle Luther had given him a package of 36 Black Cat Mega Salute firecrackers. He told the others, "We need a pipe with a cap on it. And we need to drill a hole in the cap for the fuse."

They all set off for Hunk's garage, to find a piece of pipe with a cap for their cannon. It so happened that the next door neighbor had his water heater replaced that morning, and the plumber had left the old tank and some debris including a few pieces of pipe on the curb for the trash pickup to take. Travis looked at the discarded pipe and saw just what he wanted: an eighteen-inch-long piece of one-half inch black pipe, with a cap screwed on one end.

"Great! Look at this!" he yelled. "Just what we need!"

"I know how to drill the hole," said Davie.

They took the pipe to Hunk's garage, and put the cap in a vise. Davie took his dad's electric drill from its case, inserted a 1/8th inch titanium bit, and quickly drilled a hole in the end of the cap. Jamie was the one who came up with the ammo for the cannon. He found a box of #2 pencils, and broke them in half to use as ammo. Then they all went back to the fort, with Molly and Esther tagging along behind the boys.

They immediately wanted to test the cannon. Travis unscrewed the cap, inserted the wick of a Mega Salute in the hole Davie had drilled, and then screwed the cap back on the pipe, with the Mega Salute inside. The cannon was muzzle loaded with one of Jamie's pencils and placed against a rock, aimed to the sky. Travis lit the wick and they all ran back. The cannon went off with a huge "*bang*" and the pencil went flying skyward and out of sight. The cannon was a huge success!

However, the "*bang*" from the cannon frightened Molly. She sensed that something was terribly wrong. She turned and started running away from the fort, through the field toward the house. Davie was the first to realize what Molly was doing.

"Molly's going to get mom!" he yelled.

Davie and Jamie took off running after Molly, calling her, "Molly, Molly, come! Come!!" Both boys instinctively knew they didn't want their mom to come and find they had a cannon.

Molly heard Davie and Jamie yelling. She slowed, and turned her head, as if conflicted. It was as if she knew she should get Sally, as she had when Isabella was in trouble, but being with the older children was a lot of fun. Molly stopped and turned part way around and looked back. She didn't come back, but she didn't go further toward the house either. In a moment, the two boys were beside her.

"Molly, don't run," Jamie said. "Come back to the fort with us."

Davie petted her and said, "We won't let anything hurt you. You can come back and play with us." Molly stood still for a moment, and then turned to follow the boys back.

Back at the fort, an argument ensued over where they should put the new cannon. Travis argued that they should build a rampart around the fort for protection, with the cannon on top of it.

Jamie, taking a bit of offense at the way Travis seemed to be taking over the fort, said, "Why are you deciding what we should do? We built this fort—it's ours, not yours."

"The Mexicans will come right into the fort if we don't build a wall in front of it," replied Travis. "We'll all get killed. Don't you remember what happened at the real Alamo? It had a wall around it, and the Texans held off the attacking Mexicans for 13 days. Without a wall we won't have a chance."

(Travis really meant "Texians," not "Texans," if you remember the story).

Travis ultimately convinced the others that they needed a wall around the fort, and they all went back to Hunk's garage to find shovels. There were two shovels, and trading off, the boys worked the rest of the day and the next morning building a rampart around the fort. Esther and Molly mostly just watched, but Esther did find some stones to put on the top of the wall. Building the wall was a lot of work, but it did look good. Jamie and Davie agreed it was a great addition to the fort. The boys placed the cannon on top of the rampart in front of the open part of the fort, pointed toward the grassy field.

The next day when they were all at the fort, Travis had another idea. "We need to elect a commander to make decisions when the Mexicans attack. In an army, only one person can decide what to do," he said. Then he reminded everyone that he had the Black Cat Mega Salutes and it was his idea for the cannon, and said, "That's why I should be the commander."

Jamie thought to himself: why is this guy always trying to be the boss?

He thought a moment and then spoke up, "But it's our fort!" Why should you be in charge of it just because you've got some firecrackers? Davie drilled the hole in the cap to make the cannon. And I'm the oldest, so I should be in charge!"

While Travis and Jamie argued about who should be in charge, Davie suddenly remembered the famous names from the real Alamo.

"Hey, don't you remember the guys at the Alamo?" he said. "Colonel Travis, James Bowie, and Davie Crockett!" Then he practically shouted,

"Travis, you'll be Colonel Travis. Jamie, you'll be Colonel Jamie Bowie. And I'll be Davie Crockett!"

Travis and Jamie liked the idea of being Colonel Travis and Jamie Bowie. Davie really liked being Davie Crockett, because that's who John Wayne was in the movie. They all forgot about the argument of who would be in command.

With that settled, Colonel Travis got more serious. "You know, everybody got killed at the real Alamo," he said. "The same thing could happen to us tomorrow. We need a secret weapon to beat back the Mexicans."

"What secret weapon? We don't have one," said Jamie.

"The Mexicans have to scale the rampart to get to the fort," Travis said. "Uncle Luther told me about a secret weapon that will stop 'em right in their tracks."

At this point he motioned to Jamie and Davie to come closer and then whispered in their ears, not wanting Esther to hear. Some secret mumbling then occurred among the boys, which Esther could not make out.

"OK, everybody," Travis said. "I'm getting hungry. Let's go home for lunch and then meet back here pronto."

As they started up the grassy path from the fort to the Sames house, he yelled one more instruction, "Ask for seconds, and be sure to eat all you can possibly eat!"

Jamie, Davie, Esther and Molly arrived back at the house just as Sally was finishing feeding Isabella.

They trooped into the kitchen, and Davie announced, "Mom, we're all hungry!"

Then Jamie said, "Yeah, and we all want pork and beans for lunch."

Sally, startled by this request, responded, "What, you guys have never asked for pork and beans before. Where did that come from?"

Fibbing a bit, Jamie said, "We saw pork and beans on television, and they looked really good. We all want them."

Sally not really believing this, but not much caring either, thought, OK, if the kids want pork and beans for lunch, that's it. She had two 28 ounce cans of Campbell's Pork and Beans in the cupboard. She got one out, opened it, and started heating the contents in a saucepan on the stove.

The boys ate the entire can of beans, with two slices of white bread each, washed down with milk. They were so full their stomachs hurt. Esther and Molly didn't eat beans; Esther had a bowl of fruit and a cookie, while Molly watched. Molly got only two meals a day, and that did not include lunch.

Meanwhile, Evanar and Ethelene Andersson, who lived two blocks over from Mabeley Street, were preparing to go for a walk with two of their pets. One was a chocolate Labrador retriever named Gus, who had been sent to them late the previous year by its prior owner who lived in Finland. The dog was shipped by air to Cleveland Hopkins International Airport. Evanar and Ethelene had met the flight from Helsinki to take possession of Gus at the request of Ethelene's nephew Gustave, who owned the dog but had been in a horrible accident and could no longer take care of him.

After they brought him to their home in West Jefferson, they soon found that Gus was not only strong but also very intelligent. Gus seemed to understand everything they said. The other pets they had were four champion long eared rabbits, and they were initially afraid that Gus would chase and kill the rabbits if he had a chance. But all they had to do was to tell him not to hurt the rabbits. From then on Gus not only didn't hurt the rabbits; he protected them as if they were his own. If a rabbit was out of its cage, and another dog went after it, Gus intervened in a flash. Gus never got in a fight with the other dog, but it was obvious that he in no uncertain terms told the other dog to leave the rabbit alone. And from then on, the other dog did. Gus projected that much authority.

Besides Gus, Evanar and Ethelene had decided to take Jack, their biggest long-eared rabbit, along on the walk. They put Jack on a leash, which was really the only way to control him. Gus was not on a leash. He didn't have to be, because he always did exactly what they told him to do. The four of them started out down the street on their walk. They turned the corner onto Mabeley Street, intending to walk through the field at the end of the street.

Back at the Sames' house, with lunch finished, Jamie asked his mother if they could go back to play in the fort. Sally said they could and the boys, followed closely by Esther and Molly, raced back through the grassy field past the scrubs, and into the thicket of saplings where they had built the fort. A few minutes later, Colonel Travis (they were all using their new names now) joined them, and immediately announced that they had to get ready for an attack by the Mexicans.

Excited and flushed from running through the field, his words poured out in a jumble. "I saw one of 'em back by the scrub, and I know they're more!"

"What do they look like?" asked Jamie Bowie. "How many are there?"

"I didn't get that good a look at them," responded Colonel Travis, "but I think I saw Santa Anna—he's the general—in the front. He had his horse and I think he has a donkey with him. I saw its ears. He's got a whole bunch of other Mexicans, I'm sure!"

"We gotta send out a lookout to get a better idea how many are coming," said Davie Crockett. "Esther, you and Molly go check it out!"

Esther was scared.

"Why me?" she said. "You check it out yourself."

"Santa Anna will kill all the men, but you're a girl," said Davie Crockett. "He'll let you go if you get captured."

Esther still didn't want to go.

Jamie Bowie, trying to persuade her, said, "Molly will go with you. She'll protect you if the Mexicans try to capture you."

Esther reluctantly left the fort and started down the grassy path through the field, with Molly close behind. As she followed the path, she felt more and more scared. She kept looking back at the fort. After a few minutes which seemed like an eternity, the next time she turned around the fort was out of sight. The silence was unnerving. All she could hear was the rustle of the grasses as she and Molly moved through the field. Up ahead was some of the taller scrub brush.

Suddenly Esther saw a flash of white, like a man's white shirt, on one side of some brush. It was only for an instant. Then she saw another flash of white, on the other side of the scrub brush. Then she saw a someone in a red shirt moving to the left of another scrub brush. Then she saw a red shirt to the right. She heard low voices, and froze, staring intently ahead at the brush. She turned her gaze and saw a brown animal—it had to be one of the horses Travis saw! She looked to the left, and saw something with two big ears and thought—what's that?! It's a donkey!

Esther was almost paralyzed with fear. There are hundreds of Mexicans here, she thought.

She looked down at Molly, who was sniffing the air, and said to her, in a low voice, *"Let's get out of here!"*

They both ran as fast as they could back up the path to the fort. Esther breathlessly announced that hundreds of Mexicans were advancing toward them, accompanied by brown horses and donkeys. Colonel Travis ordered Jamie Bowie to prepare the cannon. Then he gave instructions for reloading it after each shot. Finally, he told Davie Crockett and Jamie Bowie to be prepared to use the secret weapon.

"The Mexicans are going to storm the rampart, and that's when we'll beat 'em back. We'll hit 'em by surprise with the secret weapon and drive them all to Mexico! But first we'll knock some of 'em out with our cannon!"

They got ready to fire. Davie Crockett aimed the cannon in the direction where Esther said she saw the Mexicans advancing. Colonel Travis lit the fuse, as Jamie Bowie stood by to reload. The cannon went off with a huge *"bang!"* hurling its pencil ammunition in the direction of the sage brush 800 or 900 feet away.

While smoke was still wisping from the barrel of the cannon, Jamie Bowie grabbed it and unscrewed the cap from the barrel. Colonel Travis inserted the next Black Cat Mega Salute, and Jamie Bowie quickly screwed the cap back on. As he was setting it back on the rampart, Davie Crockett rammed another pencil down the barrel. The whole reloading had taken only about 15 seconds. Colonel Travis lit the fuse, and again the cannon went off with a loud "*bang*!" flinging the pencil out and into the faraway sage brush.

Evanar and Ethelene, who were walking through the sage brush with Gus and their pet rabbit, Jack, heard the first "*bang*" of the cannon. Then they heard the second "*bang*." So did the pets. Gus had smelled first Travis and then Esther and Molly, when they had been close, and dismissed them as just kids and another dog. But he did not know what this sound was. Gus cocked his head, as if trying to understand the noise he heard. Jack, the long-eared rabbit who had been mistaken for a donkey, seemed oblivious to it. He just kept jumping around, back and forth, from plant to plant, as he had been doing for the entire walk. Then a third "*bang*" occurred.

Evanar said, "Come on, we've got to find out what is going on over there!"

The four of them left the path they were on and started off in the direction of the "*bangs*" from the cannon. Just then, another "*bang*" occurred, and Evanar heard something whizz by him and land in the shrub to his right. He looked down and saw a piece of a broken, blackened pencil on the ground. That didn't have any significance to him, and they continued on. As they passed the last big scrub before entering a grassy area, the thicket of saplings with the boys' fort amongst them came into view.

Colonel Travis, Jamie Bowie and Davie Crockett all saw the advancing "Mexicans"—Evanar was wearing a white shirt and Ethelene a red shirt—at the same time.

"*Now*," said Colonel Travis. "Hit 'em with the secret weapon!!"

"What's the secret weapon?" Esther asked.

"Flamethrowers!" yelled Colonel Travis, as he pulled down his pants. He turned around with his butt facing the advancing "Mexicans," lit a match and held it between his legs. With a loud grunt he blew a huge fart! A stream of yellow/blue flame whooshed out from his butt toward the "Mexicans."

"Jamie Bowie, you're next!" he yelled.

Jamie Bowie stood on the rampart, turned around, and pulled down his pants. He lit his match as he bent over, and holding it between his legs, grunted and also ripped a huge, long fart that sent a flame streaming out over the grassy area beyond the thicket of trees.

"OK, Davie Crockett—give 'em a third blast!" he yelled.

Davie Crockett had seen both of the streaming flames sent by Colonel Travis and Jamie Bowie. He was ready, but also a bit scared.

"Won't the flame go into my butt and blow me up?!" he exclaimed.

"*No, no, no*—don't worry. Hurry, hit 'em with your flamethrower—that should be enough to scare them off and save us," Colonel Travis yelled back.

So Davie Crockett jumped up on the rampart, whirled around, yanked down his pants and lit his match between his legs, and with a huge, loud grunt blew the biggest, loudest, longest fart of the three. The flame went almost to the point where Evanar and his party had advanced, and Evanar, who was in the lead, raised his arm in front of his eyes as he saw the flame coming toward him. He lowered his arm as the flame dissipated in the sunlit air.

Ethelene grabbed her cell phone and quickly dialed 911. "Hurry," she said. "We're being shot at by huge flames!"

Evanar ran up to the fort and looked at the four kids, now scared and inside the fort.

"*What's going on here!*" he demanded.

Ethelene, who was running to keep up with her husband, got to the fort and saw the three boys with Esther with Molly behind them.

As Davie was pulling up his pants, she suddenly she realized what had happened, and said, "That's disgusting! You should be ashamed of yourselves! Where are your parents?"

Gus calmly observed the whole scene. He didn't know quite what to make of it, having never seen anything like this. He knew that Travis, Jamie, Davie and Esther were children. They seemed to him to just be playing like other children he had seen. They weren't important to him. He was more interested in Molly, who had come out from the fort wagging her tail to greet the advancing "Mexicans."

Jamie was the first of the fort defenders to speak. He walked out, stepped over the rampart, and approached Evanar and Ethelene.

"This is our fort," he said. "It's the Alamo, and we thought you were Santa Anna and a bunch of Mexicans. We thought you were going to storm our fort and kill all of us. So we shot at you with our cannon and our flamethrowers. We're sorry we scared you."

Evanar began to laugh. Then Ethelene started to laugh too.

"That's hilarious," said Evanar. "I guess we do look a little like Mexicans, I've got a white shirt and Ethelene has a red shirt. All we need is somebody else with a green shirt, and walking together we'd look like the Mexican flag."

Ethelene then said, "But you boys shouldn't play with fire. You might get hurt. With that flamethrower idea, you might blow yourselves up!"

Travis spoke up, "Oh, no, we won't blow up. My uncle Luther told me we won't. And I saw my dad spray lighter fluid from a can onto a fire; the flame never went up the stream into the can or blew it up."

Ethelene replied, "Well, I don't think it is safe. And anyway, you might set the field on fire. *That* wouldn't be safe."

At that point everyone heard a loud siren, and in a few moments a huge fire truck stopped at the edge of the field behind the thicket of saplings. It was followed by a second big fire truck, and a huge hook and ladder truck. Then a large, white Cadillac Escalade SUV with red letters announcing it was the Fire Chief's car screeched to a halt sideways in Mabeley Street, completely blocking the road. A big burly man with a fireman's hat descended from the SUV. He had blue and gold epaulettes on the shoulders of his white starched shirt, which had six rows of military ribbons. (Unknown to all but his wife, he had purchased them on-line from Medals of America for $2.89 each). On the right side of his shirt was a large badge announcing he was Chief Hickelhunt, Amberlin Township Fire Department. Then a big white Dalmatian with black spots that had been sitting in the front passenger seat jumped to the driver's seat and out of the vehicle.

"Come on, Spigot!" Chief Hickelhunt yelled. "Let's see where the fire is!" Chief Hickelhunt and his big dog, Spigot, ran to the clearing where Evanar, Ethelene, and the children were standing. They had been watching with awe as the fire trucks arrived. Gus, Molly, and the long-eared rabbit, Jack, were beside them. Gus and Molly were howling;

the sound from the sirens hurt their ears. Jack was so scared by all the noise he was shaking as he stood next to Evanar.

The seventeen firemen who had arrived before the chief had quickly observed there was no fire to be seen. They lined up behind Chief Hickelhunt. At the same time, more fire trucks and firemen continued to arrive and add to the jam of fire trucks in the street; ultimately there were twenty-seven in all.

"What's going on here?" Chief Hickelhunt demanded. "Where's the fire?!"

After hesitating a moment, Travis stepped forward and spoke first: "Sir, there isn't any fire."

"See," he remarked, looking around. "This is our play fort. It's the Alamo. There isn't any fire in it; it doesn't even have a stove." His knees were shaking a bit as he said this.

Chief Hickelhunt looked around. Obviously there was no fire; there wasn't even any scorched grass. Then, sweeping his eyes over the entire scene, he saw the pipe "cannon" and the remains of some firecrackers.

"What's this?" he demanded, while turning the eighteen-inch pipe over several times in his hands, and then looking through the "barrel" of the cannon at the hole in the cap on the other end.

Travis cast his eyes to the ground.

While Chief Hickelhunt was looking at the pipe cannon and the remains of the firecrackers, Spigot, the big Dalmatian, had discovered Molly. Spigot was a lot bigger than Molly and towered over her, sniffing her behind. Gus had already decided that he was interested in Molly, and immediately came over and in dog language, told Spigot to get lost. Spigot had to decide quickly whether to fight or back down. This was a true test of which of the two dogs was the "alpha."

However, it wasn't even close. There was no dog fight. Gus conveyed such an air of authority and dominance that Spigot left Molly and ran behind Chief Hickelhunt. He was a big dog, used to having his way with other dogs, but he was not going to challenge Gus.

Meanwhile, Travis stood with his hands in his pockets, looking at the ground. He knew he was caught. Finally, he decided to 'fess up,' and admit they had firecrackers.

"We had a few firecrackers, and we set them off in that pipe," he said. "That's all."

Chief Hickelhunt knew there was no law against having a few firecrackers. Evanar and Ethelene kept quiet; they had independently decided not to tell on the boys about the flamethrowers.

But Evanar was starting to wonder about all the fire trucks and firemen that had arrived there.

He stepped forward, and addressed Chief Hickelhunt, "I live the next street over. My wife and I were out for a walk, and I can tell you there is no fire here. I think this is all one big mistake. My wife heard the fireworks and saw the flame from the pipe the boys were using. She called 911 when she saw the flame. But there isn't any fire to put out. She never said there was one."

Then he asked, "Why are there so many fire trucks here?"

"Ahem," Chief Hickelhunt replied. "We have mutual aid pacts with all of the surrounding fire departments within 20 miles. They respond so we can be sure we provide the absolute, very best protection to you, the public."

One of the firemen, Jasper Jenkins, who was several rows back tried his best to hold in a laugh, but couldn't. He made a low "hua, hua, hua" noise which he tried to disguise as a cough.

Ethelene, who was close-by, looked over and in a low voice, asked him, "What's the matter?"

Jasper, holding back his laugh, muttered, "Sure, that's why all these fire trucks are here, like the chief said."

Then he turned to Ethelene and whispered, so no one else could hear, "It sure makes our numbers look good, when we all go to each other's fire."

Ethelene's jaw dropped. "So you mean the more fires you go to the better you look?" she said to Jasper.

Continuing to speak in his lowest tone of voice, he responded to her: "Of course. That's how we justify all the tax increases you people pay for all the fire departments around here. Everybody's afraid of a fire; it's easy to get the levies passed."

Then he added, "That's how the chief got his Cadillac."

Evanar had approached his wife and heard the last bits of this conversation.

"Well, how do you justify that hook and ladder truck? It must go up 60 feet in the air, and the tallest building allowed in this town is 35 feet. How often is it used?"

Jasper turned his head to the side before responding and again in a low voice said, "I'll deny I ever talked to you if you repeat this, but the fact is we've never used it in a fire in all of the eight years we've had it. We did use it to rescue a cat out of a tree one time."

"Pretty damn expensive cat," murmured Evanar under his breath.

As he walked away from Jasper, Evanar was still holding Jack's leash but not paying any attention to him. Jack was extremely nervous, flipping his neck back and forth, and jumping around even more than he usually did. He was scared to death of the big white dog with black spots that lay on the ground just behind the fire chief. At the same time, Spigot was entranced by Jack. He forgot about Gus; his eyes were glued on the rabbit. But then with Jack's next jerk of his head, his collar wedged up over the base of his right ear. With his next jerk to the left, it came over his neck and off of his head. Suddenly free, Jack leaped forward and began to run as fast as he could toward the field.

Spigot sprung from the ground like he was shot from a cannon. He instinctively gave chase to Jack. As he bounded up he banged into the back of Chief Hickelhunt's legs, and knocked him forward. Hickelhunt fell face down on the ground. His white starched shirt got streaked with brown dirt, and he got a cut on his chin when he hit a root with his face. Hickelhunt stood up, blood dripping from his chin onto his shirt, and started yelling for Spigot.

Evanar saw Jack take off, followed by Spigot as he knocked Chief Hickelhunt down.

Evanar turned to look for Gus, and yelled: "Save Jack!"

Gus took off in high pursuit, barking for Molly to follow. Jack, followed by Spigot, with Gus and Molly not far behind, raced the trails through the tall weeds and grasses in the field.

Now, a Dalmatian is a pretty fast dog. A typical Dalmatian is about the same height, slightly less than two feet at the shoulder, as a typical Labrador retriever, but lighter. Spigot was bigger than a typical Dalmatian, and could run very fast. But Gus was no ordinary Lab either. He could run even faster than Spigot. And he could cut on a dime. Molly, also, was an exceedingly fast runner. She was an American Lab, thinner than Gus and lanky, with long legs. She came from dogs bred for hunting, dogs that could run fast all day. So even though Spigot was a fast dog he could not outrun either Gus or Molly, even with a head start. And Jack kept zigging and zagging as he ran. He changed direction every time Spigot was just about to catch him, causing Spigot to overrun where he had just turned.

Gus and Molly quickly caught up with Spigot. Gus jumped on Spigot like a linebacker tackling a running back. With his front legs and paws wrapped around Spigot's midsection, Gus wrestled him to the ground. Molly piled on. Both Gus and Molly were on top of Spigot, who was squirming and flailing under both of them. Gus barked to Jack to "go home," and as Jack quickly disappeared, the two Labs released Spigot.

Chief Hickelhunt ran after his dog, yelling for the other firemen to help him. But the firemen from all of the other fire departments started back to their trucks to leave. They were all pretty disgusted with Chief Hickelhunt for calling them out for a false alarm, and were not about to waste any time helping him chase his dog. When they got back to their trucks, they found the street behind their trucks clogged by a long line of cars waiting to get through. Then they saw they could not go forward, because Chief Hickelhunt had driven his Cadillac Escalade SUV past the front of the first truck and then left it sideways across the road, completely blocking the road. They sat in their trucks, fuming like the trapped motorists behind them, while they waited for Hickelhunt to come back and move his SUV.

Spigot trotted back to Chief Hickelhunt and they both went back to the chief's vehicle. The firemen were all glaring at Hickelhunt from their trucks as he walked past them. He and Spigot got in the SUV, pulled it around and headed down Mabeley Street, followed by the twenty-seven fire trucks that had answered the alarm. As the street cleared, the motorists who had been trapped by this congestion finally started on their way again.

Hunk and Sally were on their way home with Isabella when they heard the sirens, and got caught up in the congestion on Mabeley Street. They parked and walked a block to their home near the end of the street. As Chief Hickelhunt and Spigot were leaving, Hunk and Sally, who was carrying Isabella, were just entering the opposite side of the field on their way to the clearing with the saplings. They came upon Evanar, Ethelene, Gus, and Jack going the other way.

"Great looking dog!" Hunk said, looking at Gus. "We have a chocolate Lab too. Molly is her name."

"We saw her!" said Evanar. "We met Molly a little bit ago. She and Gus here got along just fine; I think they like each other."

"We're on our way to see what the kids are up to," said Sally. "I hope they didn't get in any trouble."

"They're OK," replied Ethelene. "We met them too; they're pretty interesting kids, for sure. It was a little scary with all the firemen here. They'll be glad to see you."

Arriving at the clearing, Sally rushed up to the children, and asked, "What's going on? Are you all OK? Where's Molly? Was there a fire here?"

Jamie replied, "Mom, we're just fine. There's no fire. And Molly's right over here in our fort."

Hunk said, "Well, what were all those fire trucks doing?"

"Dad," Davie replied, "They just *thought* there was a fire. But there wasn't."

"Yeah," said Jamie. "We just fought the Battle of the Alamo, and we *won*! This fort here is the Alamo. We beat the Mexicans! They all left!"

Then he thought a bit, and said, "This is our friend Travis; he lives down the street. He was Colonel Travis, I was Jamie Bowie, and Davie was Davie Crockett."

Davie jumped in to the conversation, "And Travis had some firecrackers, and they scared off the Mexicans, and that's why the fire trucks came!"

Hunk said, "Well, I'm glad you all weren't in the real Alamo. I think it had a different ending. But please don't play with firecrackers anymore. You might get hurt, or set the field on fire. You can set them off when I'm around to watch."

Sally spoke up, "Travis, nice to meet you. Now, let's everybody go home for a while. Molly, you come to. I understand you have a new friend."

With Hunk in the lead, they left the clearing in front of the "Alamo." The Sames family along with Travis and Molly bringing up the rear, walked a last time that day on the path around the hills of scrub brush and through the thickets of grasses and weeds back to the house.

CHAPTER 10

PIPER'S BIRTHDAY PRESENT

That summer Molly went into heat for the third time. The previous times, Hunk and Sally had kept her isolated so no other dog could get to her. This time, they seriously considered breeding her and having puppies. They thought it would be a good experience for the children, and they also thought maybe they could make a little extra money from selling the puppies.

Even though Hunk had two jobs, money was a bit tight in the Sames household. Hunk was a biology teacher and the football coach at the high school. But his real interest was botany. That interest had led him to his second job. In the summers he worked as a pollen collector for a large drug company that made antihistamines and other over-the-counter allergy medicines. The company analyzed the pollens he collected and then developed antidotes to neutralize them.

Hunk had a pickup truck with a roof rack to carry a very tall extension ladder, which he used to harvest the pollen-laden male sex organs of the blossoms of hundreds of types of trees. This was piece-work; he was paid for each pollen sample identified with the tree it came from. He was an expert in identifying trees and he had to travel, frequently every day. Sometimes he was gone for as much as a week at a time, and sometimes the company asked him to travel to other parts of the country. When he did that, he was away from home even more. Hunk and Sally thought the money they might get from the sale of Molly's puppies could help Hunk from having to make one or two long trips away from home.

The choice of a sire was obvious. They wanted the litter to be purebred dogs, and they had met Gus, who lived two blocks away, when all the fire trucks came to the field behind their house. Gus was a great looking English Labrador retriever. They thought he would be a perfect father for Molly's puppies.

When they approached Evanar and Ethelene, they found Gus' owners were quite willing for Gus to mate with Molly. Also, they did not want one of the puppies. They had enough to do taking care of Gus as well as four long-eared rabbits. Gus needed a lot of exercise. They didn't want another dog. This meant Hunk and Sally would have one more puppy to sell. Evanar and Ethelene were sympathetic to the Sames wanting to make a little extra money, and said they would contact Gus' real owner in Finland to see if they could get his papers. If the Sames could register the puppies as purebred Labs, they would be more valuable.

Sally talked to their veterinarian about breeding Molly, and learned the signs to watch for the right time to bring Molly and Gus together. Hunk built a box for her to be in when she delivered her pups. It was comfortably bigger than Molly, and had rails on each side for the pups to get under, so Molly would not inadvertently roll over on them. They lined the box with plastic and placed newspapers on the bottom of it for the birth of the pups, called "whelping." They had towels and bath mats ready to use in the box after the pups were born. Molly was introduced to the box early in her pregnancy so she would be used to it and not pick some inconvenient place later—like the kids bath tub— to have her puppies.

The normal gestation period for a mother dog is about sixty-three days. Sally had a thermometer handy, and around that time started taking Molly's temperature. She had learned that Molly's body temperature would drop a degree or two from normal about twenty-four hours before she would give birth. When that happened, Molly also stopped eating. That evening they observed her making a nest for herself in the whelping box.

Later that evening after everyone had gone to bed, the first of Molly's pups was born. Molly tore the placental sac off of the pup with her teeth, and then severed the umbilical cord. Then she began licking the pup to stimulate its beginning to breathe. This pup was soon taking deep breaths. It then found its way to one of Molly's teats and began suckling. That let the pup ingest a milk-like fluid called colostrum, which contained Molly's antibodies produced in her mammary glands just after birth. It would help the pup fight infections in the first days of its life, before its own immune system had matured. As soon as the first pup had been born another appeared, and then another, and another, until there were ten in all. Molly was very busy, removing one placental sac after another, cleaning the pups, and stimulating them to breathe.

The children were excited about the impending birth of Molly's pups. The next morning when the family awakened, Esther was the first to run to see if Molly had given birth. She saw a bunch of squirming small puppies—she didn't know how many—in the box with Molly. Esther ran to tell her parents and her brothers and sister. Hunk and Sally looked first to see their color. They were all chocolate! Jamie started counting the puppies, but it was hard. They were crawling around, slowly, to find Molly's teats, and one got on top of another. Jamie counted nine. Esther said she saw eight. Davie said he saw ten. Later, after Hunk picked each one up to weight it on a small scale, they all agreed Davie was right—there were ten pups in all.

Molly was a good mother. The pups grew rapidly. At first, they slept whenever they were not nursing, and by the end of the week all of the puppies had doubled their birth weight. One was a little more than double in birth weight. No one in the Sames family could know, but this was the first born. Sometime after the second week, their eyes opened. They began to stand. One after another, they took their first wobbly short walk in the box. After three weeks, they started to play with each other, and venture beyond the box. At four weeks, several tried to eat a bit of Molly's food in her bowl, and Sally then started offering all of them solid puppy chow. Sharp puppy teeth soon appeared, and Molly began weaning the pups from nursing as they transitioned to solid food.

At this point, play began in earnest. There had always been a lot of activity in the Sames household, but now the children had ten puppies to play with as well. The puppies grew up with four active children carrying them around, rolling balls to them, and showing them off to their friends. When they weren't playing with the children, they were sleeping or eating or exploring a new world. One in particular, just slightly bigger than the rest (the first born) ventured all over the back yard, sniffing everything he came to.

One day when the puppies were seven weeks old, Hunk went to gather pollen from a giant Eastern cottonwood tree at one edge of a field in Delaware County, about 40 miles from home. It was a well-known tree, because it was the biggest Eastern cottonwood found so far in the state, with a trunk 370 inches in circumference and a height of 135 feet. Hunk fully extended his extension ladder against the trunk. He was careful, as he always was, in the way he positioned his ladder. However, he failed to notice a large boar on the other side of the field away from the tree. This huge boar was a Yorkshire, which is the fastest, and also the meanest breed of pigs.

This pig was not in a good mood. It wanted to mate with the female pigs that were part of the farmer's pig herd, but the pig farmer had cordoned off the females in an adjoining field to prevent that. He wanted to breed them so as to have pig litters sequentially, rather than all at the same time. The male pig could only look at the females through the fence, which made him madder and madder.

As Hunk positioned his ladder, the boar heard its "clang" against the tree. When Hunk started climbing, the boar heard his foot hit against each rung of the aluminum ladder. Attracted by the sound, the boar ran over to that side of the field. He saw Hunk and the ladder and charged. Hunk saw him coming and jumped for a branch of the tree just as the boar crashed into the bottom of the ladder, knocking it off the tree. The ladder fell to the ground with a crash. Fortunately, this frightened the boar which ran back to the other side of the field.

Hunk was now hanging from a branch about twenty feet from the ground. He struggled to get his body up onto the branch, pulling himself up with a "chin-up" and then trying to swing one leg up and over the branch. But Hunk was a big guy, and a bit overweight. Each time he tried to swing his leg up, he couldn't get it quite high enough and it slipped off the limb. He tried to get one arm completely over the branch, so he could support himself with the branch under his armpit, but he couldn't do that either. With fingers aching from holding onto the tree limb, and his biceps burning from holding his body as high as he could, his strength finally gave out and he plunged to the ground.

Hunk lay on the ground for what seemed to him forever. No one was near, noticed, or came. Fortunately, the Yorkshire boar didn't come either. Finally, moaning from the blow he had taken, Hunk slowly moved. He tried to sit up. Pain throbbed in his left arm, which he realized was broken. He began to take note of the rest of his body, and decided that he had no other broken bones. He just hurt like hell. Slowly, he got to his feet and made his way to his truck, holding his dangling left arm with his right hand.

The next day, at home with his arm in a cast, Hunk and Sally worried about how they would pay for his unexpected medical expense. Hunk wouldn't be able to work for a while, but they had the puppies. They decided they needed to try to sell them right away, even though they were young. If somebody wanted to buy one, the buyer could reserve the puppy and take it when it was nine or ten weeks old. Sally made a cardboard sign "Puppies for Sale," stapled it to a piece of lath she found in the garage, and stuck it in the ground in the front yard.

About ten minutes after Sally had put out her sign, three high school senior girls, Becky, Bobbi, and Bella (they called themselves the "ThreeBees") were driving down Mabeley Street in a yellow Mustang Bella's dad had given her on her eighteenth birthday. The ThreeBees were out joyriding after school, and the conversation (if you could call it that) went something like this:

Becky was arguing with Bobbie: "It's like, why wouldn't you text me back? I mean, you know? So, yeah, yeah, so, I was pretty upset. It's like, you know, it takes, like, two seconds. Yeah, so."

Bobbi wasn't going to take anything from Becky. She responded, "So and chill out. It's like, um, this thing, you know, like with that guy from chem class, where he was like just standing there and um, had to get to class."

"How cool is that?" replied Becky.

"That is so not cool," answered Bobbi. "You are so going to regret that. So we went down the hall, but um, he wasn't there. So like we just went back."

Bella didn't want to listen to this anymore. She started singing nonsense, in a high pitched squeaky voice, to no one in particular.

Then the thought came into her head that their friend Piper's birthday was the next day.

Her tone changed, and her voice dropped an octave: "Hey, yeah, we gotta get somthin'. Somthin' I mean for the Piper. Look, you Bees gotta stop it and think! Gotta get somthin' for the old Pipe. What'll it be? Somethin' new and cool, it's gotta be."

As they were passing the Sames house, Sally's sign caught her eye.

"Hey man di you see that!! That's what we get for the old school cat. We'll blow h'r away with a gift we'll get. Yep, yep that's it! Uppidy zing and an' hold on'a you' hat. Zing zang, flick this're thing roun zippitdy zap. Zumm zumm!!"

With that, Bella who was driving the yellow Mustang screeched close to— almost—but not quite to—a stop, as she spun the steering wheel. The Mustang slid around probably the tightest turn anyone has ever made in a Mustang, accelerated and headed back up Mabeley Street in the direction from which it had just come. Bella brought the car to a stop so sudden that the other ThreeBees— Becky and Bobbi— would have been thrown out of their seats if it had not been for their seat belts. Then they all looked to the right at the Sames house and the sign Sally had put in the front yard.

"Am I right, ladies?" said Bella.

"That's it! That's it!" Bobbi exclaimed. "We'll get her a puppy!"

"Swerve!" screamed Becky.

"Swag money!" exclaimed Bobbi.

"Can I get an Amen?" asked Bella.

"Amen, Amen," Bobbi and Becky yelled back in unison.

"*Yaaaaassss!*" replied Bella.

With that they scrambled out of the Mustang and went up to the front door.

As they rang the bell, Bella warned the others, "Hey we gotta be killin' it when we talk to these people, they may not want to giv it up to us."

"Yeah," Becky said, "Talk about the fam."

"Yeah, like mad," replied Bobbi.

Sally opened the door and looked out at the three girls. What she saw made her think, Oh, My, God! Will Esther and Isabella look like that in 12 or 14 years?!

Bella was wearing cut-off jean shorts, so short the inside pockets were showing below their front. Her top was a white lacy affair with a bare midriff. Her shoes were white platforms, with ankle straps. Bobbi's cut-off jean shorts were tie-dyed pink and black, and so tight the threads across the thighs and back were coming apart. The bottoms of the legs were so frayed they looked to Sally like they wouldn't even make a good rag. She topped it with a white singlet with the words "Van off the Wall" on a picture of a van on the front. Her shoes were pink with black laces, a slightly different shade of pink than her shorts, but nevertheless pink. Becky wore black and white shorts (hers were not frayed, nor did the pockets show), with a black fringed singlet top that exposed only a bit of her midriff. She wore black boots that came to within two inches of her knees.

Recovering a bit, Sally asked, "Can I help you?"

Bella replied, "We've come about the puppies. We want to buy one for our friend."

Becky said, "Yeah, we saw the sign. So we stopped to buy a puppy."

These weren't exactly the type of buyers Sally and Hunk had in mind for a puppy. Sally was so taken aback she was almost speechless. She couldn't think of anything to say anything other than to offer to show the puppies to the girls.

So she said, "Well, come on in. The puppies are in the back yard. We'll go out the back door and you can see them there."

They all went to the back yard. Jamie, Davie and Esther had heard them talking at the front door, and followed them out to the yard. Molly was resting under the deck which extended out about ten feet from the house. The puppies were playing in the grass. As they approached, one of the pups, slightly bigger than the rest, ran over to the three girls wagging his tail. He then started licking Bobbi's pink shoes. Then he turned around and began to pee on one of Becky's boots. Becky recoiled backward and got only a little of the pee on her boot. Then the pup started running around the yard sniffing each bush, stick and tree trunk he came to. The other pups were playing with each other, but they were obviously a bit smaller and less active.

Bella spoke first. "That's the one we want!" she said, pointing to the larger and very active pup.

Becky and Bobbi quickly agreed. "Yeah, that one for sure," Becky said.

"He is really cute!" said Bobbi. "Yeah, we want him for sure!"

Bella announced, "Yeah, and we have to take him right now, because it's for our friend's birthday."

Sally said she would have to excuse herself and talk to her husband. She went to the house, leaving the children and the girls playing with the puppies. She immediately went to the bedroom where Hunk was sitting in a chair resting with his arm in a cast supported by a strap from the ceiling.

Sally informed him: "Hunk, there are three girls here who want to buy a puppy."

"Great!" Hunk replied.

"But you should see them! I'm not sure they can take care of a puppy. But they did say they want it for a friend. And they want that pup that's the biggest. Today."

Then she added, "You know, the vet told us they should stay with Molly until they are at least eight weeks old, and this is only their seventh week."

Sally wasn't so sure about selling the pup.

Hunk pointed out that they really needed the money. "And these girls aren't the ones who are going to actually get the puppy," he said. "Why don't you ask them who they plan to give it to, and if whoever it is can take care of it?" Then he said, "Sally, I think selling this pup at seven and a half weeks is OK, because he's bigger and much more advanced than the others. If he was a kid, he'd be precocious."

Sally hesitated, but finally agreed, although she didn't feel very good about it. They did need the money, right away, and Hunk was right about how advanced this puppy was over the others. She went back to the yard and asked the girls who was going to get the puppy.

Bella, who was always the first of the ThreeBees to speak up, responded, "We have this friend, see, she's eighteen tomorrow, and see, we need to buy her a present. And this puppy is her birthday present. And she is a real cool girl, she will like it a lot."

Sally asked, "What is her name? How do we know she can take care of a puppy?"

Bobbi replied this time, "Her name is Piper. Her mom is Steffi, she's really cool and plays tennis. And her family's had dogs, they know all about dogs."

This made Sally feel better. If the puppy is going to a home that had dogs before, she thought they would be able to take care of him.

"OK," she said. "The price for the puppy is two hundred-fifty dollars. It has to be cash. Can you girls afford that?"

"Sure," said Bella. The three girls huddled for a bit, and then Bella approached Sally holding out five fifty dollar bills.

"Here is the two hundred fifty," she said. "That puppy is really cute. He'll have a good home with Piper."

Davie, Jamie and Esther had been watching the entire negotiation. They knew the puppies would be going to other homes. But now they watched as Bobbi picked up the cutest brown little puppy they had ever seen. The three girls walked around the side of the house with him, and then they heard the girls' car start up. There were nine puppies still there in the yard, but the one that had been bubbling with so much more energy was now gone. The three children looked down at the ground, and tried to hold back the tears moistening their eyes.

Piper was walking home from her after-school job as a kids dance instructor at the West Jefferson YMCA. Piper had taken ballet since age four and now as a high school senior was actually making a little money teaching younger kids what she had been doing for almost fourteen years. The kids were mostly great. The hardest part was dealing with their mothers, many of whom kept hovering around the dance room. If they thought their kid wasn't getting enough attention, Piper heard about it. And when it came time for a recital, it wasn't the kid who got the lesser part who complained bitterly, it was her mother.

Today, however, ballet class had been fun. Even the mothers behaved well. And Piper felt good about how everyone was progressing. The walk home from the YMCA seemed a lot shorter and quicker than on the days when she had to explain to an irate mother why her kid couldn't be in the front row, or mollify some other perceived slight.

As Piper approached her house, she saw Bella's yellow Mustang pull into the driveway. Then Becky, Bobbi and Bella jumped out of the car. Bobbi was holding something, but Piper couldn't make out what it was.

"*Happy Birthday!,*" yelled the ThreeBees in unison. "We got you a present!" said Becky.

"Look," said Bella, "Here he is!" And Bobbi held out her arms with the puppy in her hands for Piper to see.

"Wow, is he cute!" said Piper. "Gee, that is *so* neat! I love him, I love him, I love him!" Piper took the puppy which was squirming to get free from Bobbi and gave it a kiss.

"Woops, I think he wants to go," said Piper. She put the puppy on the ground as he was starting to pee. Then he started running around the area sniffing the grass and the nearby bushes.

Bella said, "Hey, we got to go now. Enjoy your new puppy! We'll see you in school tomorrow."

And with that, the ThreeBees jumped back into the yellow Mustang, and roared down the street.

Piper picked up the puppy and carried him into the house. Her mom was setting the table for dinner, and her dad, who had gotten home from work about fifteen minutes earlier, was in his easy chair reading the paper. Her younger brother and sister were in their rooms doing their homework. Corky, their Welsh terrier, was also upstairs, at her brother's feet.

"Hi everybody, I got a new puppy!" Piper exclaimed as she burst through the front door. "Look, isn't he the cutest puppy you ever saw!"

Piper's dad jumped from his chair. Her mother almost dropped a plate, but then caught it.

"Where did you get that puppy?!" her dad asked.

"The ThreeBees gave it to me for my birthday," Piper said. "I just got him, but I already know he is a really great puppy. Look, do you want to hold him?"

"No, Piper, I do *not* want to hold him. Look, we already have a dog. You are going to college in a little over three months. This is a small enough house for your mother and me and your brother and sister and Corky. The puppy can stay here tonight, but tomorrow morning he has to be out of here. You have to go to school in the morning, but your mother will have to take him to the pound or somewhere to find a home for him. You can't keep him, and he can't stay here."

Piper was crestfallen. The puppy had been hers for less than ten minutes, but she was already in love with him. Her dad's verdict on the puppy was like a blow to her heart.

Downcast, she said to her mother, "Maybe we better give him something to eat." Together, they went into the kitchen, Piper holding the puppy. Her mother put a small amount of Corky's dog food in a bowl and set it on the floor. Piper bent down and set the puppy on the floor next to it, and then watched as he ravenously ate all the food in the bowl.

That night Piper let the puppy sleep next to her in her bed. She understood the logic of her father's decision that the puppy had to go, but she was very worried. I wonder what kind of a home he will find, she thought to herself. I really, really hope he finds a good home.

PIPER'S BIRTHDAY PRESENT

IS LOOKING FOR A NEW HOME

<u>Coming Soon!</u>

Look for other books by Andrew Antijo in the series:

**Adventures of Deuce Clarence Jones
Book II—Fleet Athlete**

To be followed by:

**Adventures of Deuce Clarence Jones
Book III—The Alpha**

Bonus Pages!

**The following are a few pages from the beginning
of Book II in the Adventures of
Deuce Clarence Jones series**

ADVENTURES OF DEUCE CLARENCE JONES

BOOK II - FLEET ATHLETE

by Andrew Antijo

PREFACE TO BOOK II

In *Book I – The Progenitors,* three friends gave Piper a puppy as a present for her eighteenth birthday. Piper was thrilled with this cute brown puppy, which looked like a little teddy bear. However, her father was not. He told Piper in no uncertain terms that she could not keep the puppy, and that they had to find a new home for it. Piper's family had no idea of his background, or where he came from, or how special this puppy was. They had no knowledge of his progenitors, or any idea that one day he would be considered a dog prodigy—and become the greatest dog ever! All they knew was that they had to find him a new home.

CHAPTER 1

THE TENNIS CLUB

It was still dark when Piper's alarm sounded. When she crawled out of bed and turned on her table lamp, she saw the puppy was already up, exploring her room. She saw him head towards the closet, and thought, rightly, that he was probably going there to poop. Still in her nightgown, she rushed to him, picking him up just as he was bending his back legs to squat down, preparing to do his "business." Piper dashed from her room, down the stairs and to the back door carrying the puppy. She ran with him to the bushes on the side of the yard.

"There!" she scolded. "Do it there!" She left the puppy and returned to the house to brush her teeth and get dressed for school.

The kitchen was bustling. Steffi had set out cereal and fruit for the kids' breakfast and was getting ready to leave for work at the tennis club. The younger siblings ran around gathering the things they needed that day. Jeremy had soccer practice after school and couldn't find his uniform.

"What did you do with my soccer stuff!?" he yelled. His mom had washed and dried his uniform, but not yet put it back in his room.

"Look in the dryer," Steffi called back to him.

Tryouts for the eighth graders' school play were that afternoon, and Polly was going to try out for the lead part. The play was *Romeo and Juliet,* and she wanted to be Juliet. She fretted about her lines while she gathered her gown and got her makeup kit together. The gown wouldn't fit in her backpack with her books and the makeup kit. She found a grocery bag to stuff it into. Her dad, oblivious to the activity around him, was eating toast and drinking his coffee as he read the newspaper.

"Mom!" Piper cried. "We have to feed the puppy before you take him." They had agreed Steffi would take the puppy with her to work to try to find him a home.

Steffi got two bowls of dog food ready; one for Corky, their Welsh terrier, and a smaller one for the puppy. She put the larger one next to the kitchen trash can where Corky always ate, and went out the back door with the smaller one to place it on the back porch for the puppy. When she set it down he jumped up on the porch and began devouring his breakfast.

Steffi was running late. Members could make court reservations starting at 7:00 a.m. and the first group of tennis players always arrived a few minutes early. She pulled on her light white jacket while she was saying, "Goodbye! Good luck! Hope you have a good game! Hope you win the part!" to Jeremy and Polly, and then to Piper, "I won't just give him to anyone, I'll make sure he goes to a good home!" She gave her husband a rushed kiss, gathered up the puppy as she went out the door, and put him in the back seat of her old Nissan sedan.

It took only seventeen minutes to get to the Willowtree Tennis Club where Steffi worked. But she was going to be late. Steffi was the receptionist, and mornings were the busiest times. She scheduled the courts, greeted members as they arrived, told them what court they were on, answered the constant phone calls, and sold all the club merchandize, from tennis balls to clothing and new racquets. It was important that she be on time. She had already been spoken to once before for tardiness. Steffi drove as fast as she dared, her anxiety over being disciplined again building.

Beatriz, her boss, was head pro at the club. Tall, gangly, and a very good athlete, she had been the NCAA singles tennis champion her senior year in college, which was why she got her job at the club. But she had never been very successful in doubles, which requires great communication between partners who really like each other. While she was an excellent singles player, her lack of interpersonal skills prevented similar success in doubles. It also resulted in her not being a very good teacher of the sport. She especially wasn't a good doubles coach, which was terrible for the club, because most members played doubles rather than singles. She didn't seem to have a clue as to how to teach doubles strategy. Also, her style was to criticize a player's bad shots, and ignore her good shots. After a tennis lesson with Beatriz, players didn't have a lot of self-confidence, and didn't much improve their game.

The result was that when Willowtree's teams played other clubs, they usually lost. Confidence is everything in tennis, as it is in all sports. The club was beginning to lose members, and the owners were starting to put pressure on Beatriz. In turn, she was becoming even more critical of the staff. The atmosphere of the place was heavy. Since Beatriz had arrived, Steffi began to feel that it wasn't a fun place to be anymore. And she was starting to worry about her job.

So when she drove into the club parking lot, she thought she better not take the puppy into the club without asking Beatriz first. Who knows what kind of mood she might be in today, she thought. Steffi didn't want to take a chance of getting criticized and reprimanded for something that shouldn't make any difference anyway. It would only take a few moments to explain the situation to Beatriz. She braked to a hard stop in an open parking space, jumped out of the car slamming the door shut, and ran to the front entrance and up the steps that led to the lobby.

Beatriz was in her office to the left of the lobby, just in front of the hallway that led to the four courts on the left side of the building and the men's locker room.

"Morning, Beatriz," Steffi said as she poked her head in the door. "Can I see you for a minute?"

"Sure," said Beatriz, who kept scribbling on the paper in front of her on her desk, not noticing that Steffi was five minutes late. "What's up?"

"Three of Piper's friends gave her a puppy for her eighteenth birthday," Steffi said. "He's really cute, but we already have a dog, and she is going away to school this fall. We can't keep him, and I brought him with me to see if one of the members wants to take him. He's in the car. Can I bring him in?"

"Sure," said Beatriz. "Why not? Show him to me too. I've been thinking about getting a dog myself."

"Great," said Steffi, at the same time thinking that she didn't want Beatriz to be the new owner of this puppy. "I'll go get him."

The Willowtree tennis club was a great facility, with eight indoor courts, but it was old. When it was built it was in an upscale area, surrounded by subdivisions with higher priced homes occupied by people with plenty of money they could spend on club memberships. And most of the women who lived there didn't work outside the home, so they had time to play tennis during the day. Tennis was in its heyday. Andre Agassi and Jimmy Connors ruled men's tennis, and Chris Evert and Martina Navratilova were the best of the women. The sport was energized. The club boomed.

But over the years the area changed. The affluent homeowners moved further out to more distant suburbs. The upscale stores in the strip mall on either side of the main street close to the club closed their doors and were either boarded up, or taken over by merchants selling discounted merchandize or alcoholic beverages. Grocery stores closed and fast food stores opened. A number of the storefronts sported steel bars across their windows and steel door gates across their entrances. Parking lots became shopping areas for drugs at night. Crime, previously rare, flourished.

Lenny and Louie were drug pushers in the area. Lenny was the smarter of the two, and handled the business end. He got their supply of drugs from a guy named Charles. Lenny had Louie, who was a big lout, accompany him everywhere and provide "protection." The evening before Steffi went to the Willowtree with the puppy, Charles had sold Lenny two ounces of "dro," which stands for hydroponic, meaning that the marijuana was grown in water. He also sold him three rocks of pure cocaine, all on "credit." Charles expected to be paid nine hundred dollars the next day for the marijuana, and two thousand dollars for the cocaine. At street prices the marijuana should have fetched about a thousand fifty dollars. Lenny and Louie had cut the cocaine into six "eight-balls" (three and a half grams each), and expected to sell the six "eight-balls" for two thousand five hundred dollars.

But the night had been a disaster. A regular customer had passed Lenny's phone number to a guy who called himself Evander, who called Lenny to try to arrange a buy.

"Hey, are you Lenny?" the conversation started.

"Yeah, whatda ya want," Lenny responded.

"Hey man, I'm new in town, and the guy I usually hook up with is being a dick," said Evander. "So this guy I met at Abraham's gave me your number."

"Who was he?"

"Shit if I know," Evander said. "I just met him at the bar. He was real relaxed so I knew he had a good source. He was just helping me out. Now are you going to help me or what? I'll take whatever."

Lenny was always cautious when selling to a new customer. But this guy was from out of town, and sounded like he was a regular user. And he could understand the guy not knowing his customer's name.

So he answered, "OK, be in the parking lot in front of the Target on Macculloch Avenue. Eleven thirty sharp. What's your name, and what are you driving?"

"Evander. A black Buick. See you then," Evander barked into the phone, and hung up.

At eleven thirty p.m. Lenny and Louie drove into the parking lot in front of the Target. They spotted a black Buick parked at the far corner of the lot, backed against the building. Lenny pulled his old Ford Escort in parallel to the Buick, stopping so he was across from the other driver. The front of his car faced the building.

"You Evander?" Lenny asked after lowering his window.

"Yeah, whatda ya got?" said Evander.

"We got some weed and some coke. Best stuff. Really good stuff. Two dro, and six eight-balls," said Lenny.

"OK, I'm travelling. Can't get any more for a while. I'll take it all," said Evander.

"Thirty-five hundred," said Lenny. "And that's a discount from the regular price, 'cause you're taking all I got."

"OK, deal," said Evander.

At that, Lenny bent down to retrieve the drugs which he had hidden under his seat. Evander flashed his lights and immediately another car with its lights out pulled up behind Lenny, bumping against the back bumper of the old Escort and pinning it in. At the same time, a man who had gotten out of the passenger's side of Evander's Buick slipped around to the other side of Lenny's car. He pointed a pistol at Louie who was in the front passenger seat. And when Lenny looked up from retrieving his drugs he was looking into the barrel of a pistol Evander had aimed at his head.

"OK, sucker. Give me the stash. All of it! And if I have to search that piece of shit you're driving for any of it, you won't be driving again—you'll be lucky to be crawling."

Lenny and Louie handed over all of the drugs. Then they had to hand over all the money they had on them—a total of only twenty-six dollars. Evander and the car that had come up behind them sped away.

"*Now* what're we going to do?" Louie asked.

"We gotta get some cash," Lenny said. "Charles is gonna be coming after us in the morning. We gotta come up with twenty-nine hundred bucks, and quick."

So they did what they used to do before they started dealing. They drove around checking doors of parked cars to see if they were unlocked. Lenny would stop opposite a parked car and Louie would reach out and pull the door handle. If it opened, Lenny would pull up in front of the car and Louie would jump out and ransack the console and glove box looking for cash or anything of value.

They did this all night, cruising some residential streets in the more affluent areas of town. By seven a.m. they had been able to find and steal about fifteen hundred dollars in cash, and the back seat of the old Escort was packed with stolen items they thought could be sold to get more cash.

It was a few minutes after seven a.m. when they got back close to Macculloch Avenue. They passed the Willowtree Tennis Club and noticed several cars in the parking lot.

"Let's try those," said Louie.

"OK," said Lenny, as he turned into the lot of the club. He pulled next to the newest car parked there, and then the next, and then the next. All were locked, Louie reported. Then Lenny stopped next to an old Nissan.

"Bingo," said Louie. He jumped out of the Escort and ran back to the Nissan. In less than a minute, he returned and quickly got back into the front seat of the Escort.

"Nothing there," he said, "except this!" He held up a small brown puppy dog. "He was in the back seat. Looks like he might be a valuable dog!"

"What are we going to do with a dog?!" said Lenny. "And he's just a puppy." Just then his cell phone rang. He looked down at it.

"Oh, oh," he said. "It's Charles."

"Hey, Charles," Lenny answered. He turned to Louie, "Charles wants his money."

Back to Charles, "Yeah, we got some of it. We was robbed last night, but we got some."

He turned to Louie, "He said some is not enough. Charles says he wants the whole twenty-nine hundred, and he wants it now! He's over behind the Speedway two blocks away! He wants us to drive over there!"

Not knowing what else to do, Lenny drove over to and then around behind the Speedway.

Charles and one of his buddies came up to the Escort when Lenny stopped, one on each side of the car.

"OK, get your ass out of the car. Give me the twenty-nine hundred you owe me!" Charles said to Lenny, as he flipped his cigarette butt on the ground.

"Here's fifteen hundred," Lenny said, not getting out of the car. "That's all we got."

Charles' buddy pulled out a gun. Louie, who was in the passenger seat holding the puppy, saw what was happening and reached for his Glock pistol in the glove compartment. As he bent forward, the puppy, on his lap, was squeezed by his big gut. He squirmed to get free. While he was frantically pawing to get out of Louie's lap his right paw came in contact with Louie's face. Charles' buddy saw Louie reaching for the glove box, and fired into the window of the car.

BANG!

But Louie had lurched backwards when the puppy's paw scratched his face, taking the puppy back with him, and neither was hit. The bullet punched through the window, which fragmented but did not shatter throughout the car because it was safety glass. It ricocheted off of the front window pillar on the other side of the car with a loud "clang," and flew out the window past Charles' right ear taking with it half of his ear lobe.

Charles screamed in pain. *"YOU DUMB ASS!!* He yelled. "You shot off my ear!" He dropped his gun as he slammed his right hand against his bloody ear.

A second later his gun discharged as it hit the ground.

BANG!

The gun was pointing toward the back of Charles' car when it hit the ground and fired. The bullet just missed the rocker panel under the right rear door of the car and hit the underside of the gas tank. Gasoline streamed from the bullet hole in the tank.

Louie was again reaching for his Glock in the glove compartment just as Charles started screaming. He grabbed it and returned fire on Charles' buddy.

BANG! BANG!

But as Charles' buddy saw Louie about to shoot, he had jumped backwards, tripping over his own feet. Louie's shots missed as the other man fell to the ground. When he hit the ground, he rolled around and then pulled off six shots into the side of the car.

BANG! BANG! BANG! BANG! BANG! BANG!

At that moment the gasoline streaming from the hole in the gas tank reached the cigarette butt Charles had flipped to the ground. The gasoline ignited and flames flashed back to and under the car. Then the gas tank exploded!

BOOM!

The whole back of the car was suddenly in flames. A huge smoke cloud began filling the air. Charles, who was closest to the flaming car, scrambled to the front of the Escort.

Sirens were deafening as three police cars roared to the scene. The first to arrive screeched to a halt behind the Speedway no more than ten feet behind the Escort. The first thing the officer did was to call for the fire department. His cruiser was joined moments later by another which jolted to a stop beside it. Officers from both cruisers jumped from their cars, each with both arms straight out aiming their pistols at Charles and his buddy.

"Drop your guns and put your hands over your heads!" they ordered.

Lenny and Louie, who was still holding the puppy, both sat still inside the Escort. Each eased down in his seat, as if they thought by doing that they would not be seen. Charles and his buddy were quickly handcuffed. A third officer who had just arrived at the scene approached the Escort and ordered Lenny and Louie to get out with their hands up.

Lenny got out of the car with his hands up, but Louie stayed in his seat.

"I can't put my hands up," yelled Louie. "I'm holding this puppy!"

The officer looked in the car and saw Louie holding the puppy. He turned to the other officers, who now had Charles and his buddy each locked in the back seat of one of the patrol cars.

"I just had a call come in on the radio that a brown puppy was stolen over at the Willowtree," he said.

He turned back to Louie, aiming his pistol at him, and ordered: "Get out and give me that puppy. Where did you get him, anyway?"

Louie got out of the car holding the puppy, which was still squirming. He knew he was caught.

"Yeah, we did get him at the Willowtree," he said as he handed him over.

"Here, little guy," the officer remarked as he took the puppy from Louie. At that point four more cruisers and two fire trucks were pulling into the lot. "I'll take you back home," he said, looking at the puppy.

Then he turned to the other officers, "The Willowtree Tennis Club is only two blocks away. You guys have enough back up now. I'll return this puppy and be right back."

The officer who now had the puppy thought to himself, geeze, this is really a beautiful puppy. If someone over there doesn't claim him, I'm going to keep him myself. But he did go to the club to see if somebody would.

The puppy had been gone from the Nissan for less than twenty minutes when at 7:30 a.m. the officer walked into the lobby of the club.

He inquired, "Does this puppy belong to anyone here?"

Steffi jumped up from behind the main counter.

"Yes!" she said. "He's my puppy. Oh, God I'm so glad you found him! I have no idea what happened to him. Thank you so much for finding him."

"No problem, Ma'am. That's what we're here for, to serve."

"That was so quick; I just reported him missing less than fifteen minutes ago. I guess he didn't experience any trouble."

"No, not really."

"Well, can you tell me what happened?"

"Uh, he just got taken by some drug dealers and then got mixed up in a gun battle and a car fire. Nothing really serious, gas tank just exploded."

"Oh my God!" Steffi said. "Is he OK?"

"Yes, ma'am. No trouble at all. He seems like a really good puppy. Nothing seemed to bother him. He didn't cry or nothin."

"Really? Well ..." Steffi didn't know what to say.

Finally, she replied, "Yeah, he's a really good puppy. You know, he's not even eight weeks old yet."

And with that, the officer turned and went back to his cruiser.

Steffi said to herself, yeah, he really is, he really is a good puppy. I sure hope nothing else happens before he finds a home. She put the puppy on the floor and turned back to her desk.

The puppy began running around the lobby, sniffing everything he came to. Then he saw an open doorway and ran into Beatriz' office....